Flying Saucers from the Earth's Interior

Raymond Bernard

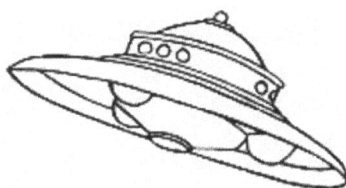

SAUCERIAN PUBLISHER

ISBN:**9781955087049**

© 2022, Saucerian Publisher

PROLOGUE

It is generally a good idea to return to the classics in any genre. This also goes for UFO literature. Rereading a book, or reviewing old documents after ten or twenty years is a rewarding experience. You will discover new data and ideas you didn´t notice before. The reason, of course, is that you are, in many ways, not the same person reading the book the second or third time. Hopefully you have advanced in knowledge, experience, intellectual and spiritual discernment. A good starting point is to reread the contactee classics material of the 1960s, in order to understand the deeper mystery involved in what happened during that era.

Raymond Bernard claims that there is evidence from Arctic explorers concerning the existence of a Hollow Earth with openings at the poles into which Admiral Byrd, the Columbus who Discovered a New World, entered a land of mountains, forests, lakes, and rivers, greenery, a mysterious land beyond the pole. According to the author, the flying saucers are the super-race vehicles that live in this vast underground world.

Saucerian Publisher was founded to promote Flying Saucer, Paranormal, and the Occult books. Our vision is to preserve the legacy of literary history by reprinting editions of books that have already been exhausted or are difficult to obtain. Our goal is to help readers, educators, and researchers by bringing back original publications that are difficult to find at a reasonable price while preserving the legacy of universal knowledge. This title is an authentic reproduction of the original Bernard's *Flying Saucer from the Earth's Interior,* initially published in 1964. This book is a facsimile reproduction of the original printed text in shades of gray. Because this material is culturally important, we have made it available as part of our commitment to protect, preserve and promote knowledge in the world.

IMPORTANT,although we have attempted to maintain the integrity of the issues accurately, the present reproduction could have missing and blurred pages poor pictures due to the age of the original scanned copy. Because this material is culturally important, we have made it available as part of our commitment to protect, preserve and promote knowledge in the world.

Editor
Saucerian Publisher, 2022

FLYING SAUCERS

from the

Earth's

INTERIOR

By Raymond Bernard, A. B., M. A., Ph. D.

GLOBE SHOWING SECTION OF THE EARTH'S INTERIOR

The earth is hollow. The poles so long sought are but phantoms. There are openings at the northern and southern extremities. In the interior are vast continents, oceans, mountains and rivers. Vegetable and animal life are evident in this new world, and it is probably peopled by races yet unknown to the dwellers upon the earth's exterior.

THE AUTHOR.

Reproduced from "The Phantom Of The Poles" by William Reed, published by Walter S. Rockey Company, New York, 1906.

FLYING SAUCERS

From the Earth's Interior

Evidence from Arctic Explorers Concerning the
Existence of a Hollow Earth with Openings
at the Poles into which Admiral Byrd,
the Columbus who Discovered a New World,
penetrated for 2300, entering a Land of
Mountains, Forests, Lakes, Rivers,
Greenery and Animal Life - the
Mysterious Land Beyond the Pole

By Dr. Raymond Bernard
(A.B., Columbis University, M.A., Ph.D., New York University)

WHERE DO FLYING SAUCERS COME FROM?

There are two major theories regarding the origin of the flying saucers: (1) the theory that they come from other planets, and (2) the theory that they come from inside the earth.

For some years the former theory was the most popular one, and many books came out about "space ships". Recently, however, foremost authorities on flying saucers, as Ray Palmer, editor of "Flying Saucers" magazine, are inclining to the view that they come from the hollow interior of the earth, coming out through the polar openings. In the following pages we shall present scientific evidence in favor of this latter conception as against the belief that flying saucers come from other planets.

There is not a particle of evidence in support of this theory of the planetary origin of the flying saucers. We shall attempt to show in the following pages that it is false, and that the true origin of the saucers is an advanced civilization existing INSIDE THE EARTH! For, rather than being solid as was formerly supposed, the Earth has a hollow interior with openings at the poles through which saucers fly back and forth between the external and the internal atmosphere of the Earth.

In support of this conception is the remarkable experience of Admiral Byrd, who flew for 1700 miles beyond the Pole and into this opening, where it became warmer the further he went in, observing forests, lakes, rivers, animals and green vegetation, and the fact that a mass visitation of flying saucers took place right after the Hiroshima atomic explosion, which is much better explained on the basis of the theory that they come from the interior of the Earth than that they come from other planets. People of other planets would certainly be less worried about the effects of atomic explosions in poisoning our atmosphere than inhabitants of the Earth's interior, who derive their air from the outside (through the polar openings). Also if visitors from other planets came here for purposes of observation, they would not send regular fleets of flying saucers traveling in mass formation, obviously to attract our attention, nor would flying saucers have such a predilection for our military airports, to be observed by members of the Air Force.

The reasons for these facts are as follows: Fearing that continuance of atomic explosions, especially in event of a nuclear war, would poison the external atmosphere sufficiently to dangerously pollute the internal atmosphere inside the Earth's hollow center, to constitute a peril to the lives of the inhabitants who depend on it for their existence, the Subterranean People, as soon as the news of the Hiroshima atomic explosion reached them, sent up fleets of their flying saucers in order to prevent such a catastrophe, which would annihilate inhabitants on the outside of the Earth's crust as well as those who live on the inside. To accomplish this, they decided to make their existence known to surface inhabitants by coming conspicuously in fleet formation, so as to attract as much attention as possible. Also, since reports from the Air Force would be taken more seriously by Government leaders than those coming from laymen, flying saucers purposely came near military airports, as in the case of the

1

famous Captain Mandell incident, when an Air Force officer chased a
flying saucer until his plane exploded.

The purpose of all this was the following. By terminating the
traditional secrecy that hid their existence from the eyes of surface
dwellers and by convincing them that they are members of a super race
whose scientific development is vastly beyond our own, the Subterranean People hoped to later arrange meetings between their scientists
and our Government leaders in order to convince the latter to immediately stop further nuclear explosions and to destroy all atomic
weapons.

But the plan failed. Instead of recognizing their existence as
a superior race coming to help us, and in spite of the undeniable
evidence possessed by the Air Force, the U.S.Government refused to
acknowledge the existence of the flying saucers or to cooperate with
their efforts to avert a world catastrophe. Instead, military planes
pursued flying saucers when they came near military airports, obviously
with intention to open fire on them and down them, in order to discover the secret of their source of power. Disappointed with their
efforts to befriend and help surface humanity, the leaders of the
Subterranean People withdrew the fleets they formerly sent up so
enthusiastically during the early period of flying saucer visitation,
leaving just a few scouts in our atmosphere to conduct fallout measurements, so that subterranean scientists could adjust their air purifiers
to cope with the increased concentration of radioactive dust in the
air passing from the external to the internal atmosphere through the
polar openings.

The above seems to be a much more reasonable explanation of the
origin of the flying saucers and the reason for their visitation
following the explosion of the first atomic bomb in Hiroshima in 1945
than the interplanetary hypothesis, which leaves many questions un-
answered. First of all, those who claim that flying saucers came
from other solar systems cannot explain how they could have arrived
here so soon after this atomic explosion took place, since other solar
systems are many light years away, and it would take years for the
flash of the explosion to reach them. Also, why should they be so
worried about atomic explosions on earth, even if they would eventually
poison our atmosphere, for this could not affect them in any way?
On the other hand, it certainly would endanger the inhabitants inside
the Earth's hollow interior, who had sufficient reason to send their
fleets of flying saucers up to befriend us in order to protect themselves by convincing us to stop further nuclear explosions.

But there are many other arguments against the interplanetary
hypothesis of the origin of the saucers. It does not explain how,
under entirely different geological, chemical, atmospheric, gravitational, climatic and other conditions, planets millions of miles away
could develop living beings so much like us in structure, appearance,
language and ideas as the "Venusians", for example, that Adamski met
in the "space ship" he visited.

Ever since H. G. Wells wrote his "War of the Worlds", it was
generally believed both by scientists and science fiction writers
that people of other planets were entirely different from us in
structure, psychology, language and in every other characteristic.
Wells depicted Martians as mechanical monsters. It was generally

2

believed that it would be a rare coincidence that other planets would develop forms of life similar to the human form as this planet has done, but rather other strange creatures entirely unlike us.

Perhaps that is why, when saucermen were described by observers as not only looking like us, having a stature similar to our own, and even speaking our language without a foreign, or rather "interplanetary" accent, these reports were considered as fantastic or fraudulent by the scientific world, and rightfully so, since it is inconceivable that inhabitants of other planets could be so much like us as saucermen seem to be. And when Adamski described the reception he was given during his visit to a Mother Ship, where he was received and treated as he would be in the drawing room of some high class hotel, the similarity between the appearance, social behavior, language, ideas and mannerisms of the so-called "Venusians" and ourselves should start us wondering and questioning.

It seems much more likely that the people Adamski and other observers saw and met, who claimed to have come from other planets, were really members of our own terrestial race who had transferred residence to the Subterranean World in the hollow interior of the world, and were employed by these people as flying saucer pilots, under orders to never reveal their Great Secret and to pretend that they came from other planets and that their craft is a "space ship". The reason for this is obvious, and the same as the reason why the surface world has been kept in almost total ignorance of the existence of a superior civilization and a super race, far beyond us in its scientific development, inhabiting the hollow interior of the earth. The reason is that the land area of this New World is greater than on the surface, where the area occupied by ocean water is greater, and that if surface governments learned of the existence of this new territory, not recorded on any map, they would make a mad rush to be the first to acquire it. They would forget their race into space and instead start a race into the hollow interior of the earth, sending armies of ice breakers and military forces equipped with atomic weapons into the "land beyond the Pole", where, as Admiral Byrd reported there is green vegetation, mountains, lakes, rivers and animal life. This would lead to a war among the rival nations trying to claim this territory first, and a still worse war between the surface people and the Subterrean People. The former would use atomic weapons, while the latter would use a form of energy at their command more destructive than atomic energy, known as "vril", which they project in the form of Death Rays, which cause atomic disintegration and the transformation of matter into energy or radiations, causing their attackers to disappear.

But the Subterranean People are pacifists and vegetarians, as Bulwer Lytton correctly described them to be in his "The Coming Race"; and it was to avoid such a war that they kept their existence and whereabouts a secret and ordered all flying saucer pilots to pretend that they came from Mars, Venus or other planets out in space and that they were "spacemen" traveling in "space ships". And gullible people who contacted them accepted their bluff.

If some flying saucers came from inside the Earth then there is every reason to believe that they all did, for otherwise it would be far-fetched to assume that the mass visitation that followed the Hiroshima explosion was composed of both visitors from inside the

3

earth and visitors from outer space who all arrived at the same time. Did they previously communicate with each other by extra long distance radio telephone and arrange to meet here at this time? If so, those who came from other planets would have to time their date of departure so that they arrived simultaneously with those who come from inside the earth, who required just a few hours' travel at most.

That would be preposterous! Either they all came from other planets or all came from inside the earth. And if they came from different planets and all arrived at the same time, a similar situation would arise whereby they would have to leave at different times to all arrive simultaneously. And why should they come? Can we imagine that superior beings who were advanced enough to build flying saucers have nothing to do but make foolish trips through space in order to take some flying saucer writers on trips to their planet? If they were so advanced in scientific development to be able to create flying saucers then they should also have telescopes so powerful that they could behold what was happening here without the need to send fleets of space ships here.

If they come for purposes of observation, a single interplanetary super-Sputnik with television transmitters could do the job. All these arguments militate against the theory of the interplanetary origin of the flying saucers. We are left with one and only one conclusion: SAUCERS COME FROM THE EARTH'S INTERIOR AND FROM NO OTHER PLACE! If some came from there during the post-Hiroshima visitation then they all came from there at this time. We cannot believe that saucers from various parts of the universe, as well as from inside the Earth, held a Cosmic Reunion in our atmosphere right after the Hiroshima explosion by prearranged appointment. If so, some of them would have to have left before the explosion occurred in order to arrive here at the same time as the subterranean saucers which left soon after!

In the following pages the author hopes to smash to pieces the popular idea that saucers come from other planets-an idea fit only for teenage readers of science fiction magazines, and unworthy of a mature intelligence, and to present scientific evidence to prove that (1) the Earth has a hollow interior with openings at the poles, and (2) the flying saucers originate in this hollow interior, where lives a super race whose scientific development is vastly ahead of our own. You may now ask: "If such a race exists there, why do our scientists know nothing about them?"

The answer is obvious. They regard us as "mechanized barbarians" whom it would be dangerous to contract or to inform of their existence, for which reason the saucer pilots they sent up were instructed to pretend that they were "spacemen" who came on "spaceships" from other planets. By means of this bluff, which so many flying saucer "experts", as Adamski and the rest, gullibly swallowed, the Subterranean People guarded the secret of their whereabouts so that no power-mad militarists would send an army of ice crackers through the North Polar opening with intention to invade and attack them and force them to project their Death Rays that would disintegrate the atoms of which their would-be attackers were composed and cause them to disappear.

SCIENTIFIC EVIDENCE THAT THE EARTH IS HOLLOW WITH OPENINGS AT THE POLES

In 1906, Walter S. Rockey Company of New York published a re-markable book by William Reed entitled "The Phantom of the Poles". This book deserves far more attention than it received. It seems to have been deliberately suppressed by those who had a special reason why the information it contains regarding "the land beyond the Pole" should not be made public. Reed offers the following bibliography, containing reports of Arctic explorers, in confirmation of his theory that the Earth is hollow in its interior and not solid as commonly supposed and that there are openings through the crust at the poles, which connect the hollow interior with its outer surface: "Three Years of Arctic Service", Charles Scribner's Sons, New York, "Northward", F.A.Stokes Co., Copyright 1902, Rockwood, New York, "Farthest North", copyright 1897 by Harper and Brothers, New York.

"IN CONCLUSION" Page 282 - Quoted in Full

"The earth is either hollow or it is not. What proof have we concerning the latter? Not one iota, positive or circumstantial. On the contrary, everything points to its being hollow. If it be so, and there are burning volcanoes in the interior, would you not see great lights reflected on the icebergs and the clouds, just as other great fires reflect the light? Would not great clouds of smoke and dust be seen - the same as from any other burning volcano? That is what all the explorers have witnessed - low dark clouds rising from the ocean, or at the edge of the ice. Nansen (an Arctic explorer) said: "Let us go home! What have we here to stay for? Nothing but dust, dust, dust!"

"Where could such dust come from - so bad that it was one of the great annoyances in the heart of the Arctic Ocean, if it did not come from an exploding, burning volcano?

"If the earth be hollow, would it not be warmer in winter and cooler in summer (as we enter the polar opening?) Arctic explorers say that a north wind in winter raises the temperature, while a south wind lowers it. As an opposite fact, in summer a south wind raises the temperature and a north wind lowers it. That is just what would occur if the winds come from the interior of the earth. Again, if the earth is hollow, it could not be round, inasmuch as the opening would take from its roundness in proportion to the size of the opening. All now agree that the earth is flattened at the poles. Also it is warmer the farther one goes north or south. Why is this the case?

"There is but one answer, and that is that the earth is hollow, and is warmer in the interior than on the exterior. As the wind passes out in the winter, it warms the atmosphere. If the earth be solid, neither science no reason furnishes any rational theory why it should be warmer as one passes north. Every known theory is against such a conclusion. As soon as you adopt the belief that the earth is hollow, perplexing questions will be easily solved, the mind will be satisfied, and the triumph of sensible reasoning will come as a delight never to be forgotten.

INTRODUCTION

"This volume is not written to entertain those who read for amusement, but to establish and prove, so far as proof can be established and proved, a half-score or more of mighty truths hitherto not comprehended. This may seem boastful, but when understood, I hope it will not be so considered, for one key will unlock them all.

"The problems to be solved are as follows:

"1. Why is the earth flattened at the Poles?

"2. Why have the Poles never been reached?

"3. Why is the sun invisible so long in winter near the farthest points north or south?

"4. What is the Aurora Borealis?

"5. Where are the icebergs formed and how?

"6. What produces the many tidal waves?

"7. Why do meteors fall more frequently near the Poles and from where do they come?

"8. What causes the great ice pressure in the Arctic Ocean during still tide and calm weather?

"9. Why is there colored snow in the Arctic region?

"10. Why is it warmer near the Poles than 600 to 1,000 miles away from them?

"11. Why is ice in the Arctic Ocean frequently filled with rock, gravel, sand, etc.?

"12. Does the compass refuse to work near the Poles?

"Should I be able to give reasonable answers to the above questions - replies that will satisfy any intelligent person - the public will admit, I believe, that I have fulfilled my task. Above all, I hope to be exonerated from trying to make others believe things in which I place no credance. So sure am I that my solutions of the problems given are correct that I am willing to stake all on their correctness. To me, the solutions given in this volume are perfectly clear. I have thought over every possible objection, and all statements are presented with certainty.

"They have been taken up under separate heads, and thus furnish the reader with what the lawyers would term a brief, giving authorities on whose statements I base my opinion. The judges, in this case, will be the public, whom I hope to have on my side.

"Before I do this I wish to acknowledge my indebtedness to the brave men who have spent their time, comfort and many, their lives, that all might know the truth and the geography of this wonderful world. Through their reports, I am able to prove my theory that this earth is not only hollow, or double, but suitable in its interior to sustain man with as little discomfort as on its exterior, and can be made accessible to mankind with one-fourth the outlay of treasure, time and life that it cost to build the subway in New York City. The number of people that can find comfortable homes (if it be not already occupied) will be billions.

GENERAL SUMMARY (Page 20)

"I claim that the earth is not only hollow, but that all, or nearly all, of the explorers have spent much of their time past the turning point, and have had a look into the interior of the earth. When Lieutenant Greely was beholding the mock sun at 120 degrees latitude, he was looking into our sister world; and when Nansen saw the square sun lined with horizontal bars, he was gazing at what may be the future home of his daughter, then two years old.

"1. Why is the earth flattened at the Poles? As the earth is hollow, it could not be round, is the answer to that. Again, the opening to the interior would detract from its roundness just in proportion to the size of the opening.

"2. Why have the Poles never been reached? No Poles exist, in the sense usually understood. The term, "the Poles", will be used throughout this work, however, for convenience sake, as covering the farthest point from the equator, so long sought for by diverse explorers.

"3. Why does the sun not appear for so long a time in winter near the supposed Poles? Because during the winter the sun strikes the earth obliquely near the Poles. Upon the way round the curve, approaching the interior, the earth becomes hollow, and one sinks a long way in. Hence the sun shines over him; it does not show up again until it strikes that part of the earth more squarely and shines down into the basin.

"4. Assuming that the earth is hollow, the interior should be warmer. We will produce what evidence we can to show that it is warmer. The ones that have explored the farthest will be the best judges.

"5. We must now resort to the compass. Does it refuse to work when drawing near the supposed Poles?

"6. Meteors are constantly falling near the supposed Poles. Why? If the earth be solid, no one can answer this question. If hollow, it is easier answered. Some volcano is in eruption in the interior of the earth, and from it rocks are thrown into the air. (Magnetic influences may attract the meteors toward the polar region - transcriber's note.)

"7. Vast quantities of dust are constantly found in the Arctic Ocean. What causes this dust? The volcanic eruptions. It has been analyzed and found to be carbon and iron, supposed to come out of some volcano.

"8. What produces the Aurora Borealis? It is the reflection of a fire within the interior of the earth. (Transcriber's note: The Aurora Borealis may be due to rays from the central sun in the center of the earth as reflected on the night sky above the North Polar opening. Why are there Northern Lights but no "Southern Lights"? Does this not mean that the South Polar opening through earth's crust is closed by the ice of the frozen continent of Antarctica?)

"9. Where are icebergs formed? And how? In the interior of the earth where it is warm, by streams or canyons flowing to the Arctic Circle, where it is very cold, the mouth of the stream freezing and the water, continuing to pass over it, freezing as it flows. This prevails for months, until, owing to the warm weather in summer, the warmth from the earth, and the warm rains passing down to the sea, the bergs are thawed loose and washed into the ocean. Icebergs cannot be formed on earth, for the reason that it is colder inland than at the mouth of a stream. Hence the mouth would be the last to freeze and the first to thaw. Under these conditions, icebergs cannot be formed.

"10. What causes tidal waves in the Arctic? Many are started by icebergs leaving the place where they are formed, and plunging into the ocean. This answer is given because nothing else can produce one hundredth part of the commotion of a monster iceberg when it plunges into the ocean. (Transcriber's note: Except an underwater volcanic explosion which is rare compared to the tidal waves reported in the Arctic by the explorers and which are frequent.)

"11. What causes colored snow in the Arctic region? Two causes: The red, green and yellow are caused by a vegetable matter permeating the air with such density that when it falls with the snow it colors it. This vegetable matter is supposed to be the blossom or pollen of a plant. As it does not grow on earth, one can naturally believe that it must grow in the interior. Black snow is caused by black dust, consisting of carbon and iron, and supposed to come from a burning volcano. As no burning volcano is near the Arctic Ocean, it also must come from the interior of the earth.

"12. Why are the nights so long in the Arctic region? In winter, the sun strikes the earth obliquely in that locality, and in approaching the Poles, one passes down into the hollow, thus shutting out the sun until it strikes the earth more squarely.

"13. What causes the great ice pressure in the Arctic Ocean during still tide and calm weather? One of the great annoyances, as well as dangers, met with in the Arctic regions is the ice-pressure. This is caused by different conditions. Reference is not made to hummock or loose ice that grinds against the shore, or fast ice, but to the ice that ships get fast in and drift with. Ice-pressure arises from change of current caused by the tide setting in or out, a strong wind with a sudden change, and in calm weather, the tidal wave, most annoying of all, for it comes when not expected, and turns everything topsy turvy. The ice, accordingly, has no show and must break. A wind is different. The whole moves along like a monster raft. The sea is covered, and cannot rise, while the wind blows a perfect gale. This, when under cover in ship or hut, is but little felt; but when a tidal wave puts in an appearance, things are different. The wave is in motion long before it reaches the ice-field, and the force that keeps it moving is not interfered with by the ice, which is lighter than the wave, else it would sink. When the ice, therefore, is raised it must break, split and roar, but the wave goes on.

"14. Why is the ice filled with rock, gravel and sand? These substances came from an exploding volcano near where the iceberg was formed. As they fall during all seasons of the year, they appear, of course, in all stages, from the time the stream first froze over until the iceberg passed into the ocean."

On page 26 is a picture of the globe showing an artist's conception of the earth's interior. Below the picture, it reads:

"The earth is hollow. The Poles so long sought are but phantoms. There are openings at the northern and southern extremities. In the interior are vast continents, oceans, mountains and rivers. Vegetable and animal life are evident in this new world, and it is probably peopled by races yet unknown to dwellers upon the earth's exterior."

Chapter I is only three pages in length, and shows that the earth, being admittedly flat at the Poles, is in the right shape for it to have openings in the Arctic and Antarctic regions.

Chapter II summarizes the experience of the explorers who very quickly passed from the region of sunshine into the region of long nights, or the opposite. The sun there is absent for abnormally long periods of time, which could not be the case if the earth was round or even just slightly flattened at the Poles. The only explanation is that these explorers entered into the opening at the North Pole; and as they entered, the sun's rays were cut off from them, to reappear only when it was high enough in the sky to shine in. Nor did they penetrate far enough to receive the rays of the interior, smaller sun in the center of the earth.

Chapter III is devoted to the working of the compass as observed by all the explorers who got very far north and that this strange action of the compass is exactly what should be the case if the earth is hollow. An excellent drawing of a cross-section of the opening with ships sailing both in and out had this caption under it: "This illustration is presented to show how the magnetic needle works in passing into the interior of the earth, and how the compass would lead explorers out again, they not knowing the earth was hollow!" We now quote Reed's words:

"WORKING OF THE COMPASS. If the earth be hollow, what is expected of the compass? Anyone knowing anything about a compass knows that as soon as a ship begins to turn, the needle will tip up as far as it can. To satisfy himself, let the reader take any compass and tip it toward the south. The needle will drop as far as it can. Then tip it north, and see how quickly it will rise to the glass on top. If the compass will work like that in New York, why should it not do the same near the Poles? As soon as the curve begins, which is probably about 55 to 60 degrees latitude, the compass will try to follow north, and, in order to do so, will rise to the glass at the top, as far as the adjustment permits.

9

"Greely proved that when the needle was suspended on an untwisted silken thread, it stood pointing nearly straight up. That was at latitude 85 degrees; at 90 degrees it would be erect. That is just what would be expected if they were nearly at the turning, or at the farthest north point. On the explanation that the earth is hollow, the needle worked just as it should have and if it worked differently, would have been wrong.

"A compass, or magnetic needle, is controlled by one of the laws of the universe, and when in order works accurately. If it does not seem right, it is better to halt and see if the fault be not elsewhere. The fact that the compass does not work, as some believe that it should, is one of the strongest arguments in favor of the theory that the earth is hollow, for had it pointed to the supposed north, it could well be claimed that if the earth was hollow, the needle would not have pointed as it did. What seems therefore to be a defective compass, turns out to be one of the powerful proofs necessary to substantiate a great truth.

"As Greely's trip was for scientific purposes, great attention was paid to every branch of it. Let us note right here the observation of the magnetic needle, and see if we can account for the unruly conduct of this little metal servant that has always proved such a faithful friend of man. If the earth be hollow, and sailing in a direction that seems to be north - but, as a matter of fact, down - while holding that course, you will sail round the farthest point north, you gradually pass into the interior, and your head will soon be toward the north and your feet toward the south. This would be the exact position when a ship or individual is halfway in or around the curve. The needle would then have to point straight up. Whay did it do. Greely says on page 127:

"'For the uninitiated, it should be said that the object of these readings was to note the declination of the magnetic needle. In the greater part of the world, the compass does not point to the geographical pole, and the saying, 'true as the needle to the pole', is only an inaccurate simile. The magnetic declination of any place is the difference between the geographical pole and the quarter to which the needle actually points, and is measured in degrees to east or west. For instance, where the needle points to the true west, the declination is said to be 90 degrees W., and when pointing to the southwest, to the 135 degrees W. At Fort Conger, in 1882, the magnetic needle pointed between the west and southwest, the declination being 100 degrees 13 minutes W. In the magnetometer, a small magnet freely suspended by a single fibre of untwisted silk swings readily in any horisontal direction. This magnet at Conger was never quiet, nor even on what are technically known as calm days, but swung to and fro in a restless, uneasy way, which at various times impressed me with an uncanny feeling quite foreign to my nature. As it swung to right and left, its movements were clearly outlined on a fixed glass scale, which served as a background, and the extreme oscillations, seen through a small telescope by the observer, were recorded. In the other end of the building was placed, on a stable pier, a dip-circle, from which the linclination or dip of the magnetic needle was hourly determined. A magnetic needle, nicely and delicately balanced, in the middle latitudes, assumes a nearly level position. At Conger, however, the needle, adjusted so that it can move freely in a vertical plane shows a strong tendency to assume an _upright position_. At a dip of 90 degrees, the needle would be erect. While at Conger, the inclination was about 85 degrees.'"

Comment of Reed: "What made the needle so restless? So much so that it caused Greely such unpleasant emotions? If that needle was suspended in the middle latitudes, it would, as he said, assume nearly a level position. Let us see why it takes that position, and perhaps we can then tell why it assumes a different position when nearing the Poles. It takes the level position because gravity draws it down and the magnetic pole swings it round. When one is entering the curve of the earth, the magnetic pole pulls one end of the needle up, toward a perpendicular position.

"By treating the earth as hollow, we have the solution of all the great mysteries - such as tidal waves, ice-pressure, colored snow, open Arctic Ocean, warmer north, icebergs, flattening of the earth at the Poles, and why the Poles have not been found, the supernatal giving way to the natural, as it always does with understanding, and relief comes to mind and body.

"In Volume II, pages 18 and 19, Nansen writes about the inclination of the needle. Speaking of Johansen, his aide, he says: "One day - it was November 24th, he came in to supper a little after six o'clock, quite alarmed, and said, 'There has just been a singular inclination of the needle to twenty-four degrees and, remarkably enough, its northern extremity pointed to the east. I cannot remember ever having heard of such an inclination." He also had several other inclinations of about fifteen degrees. At the same time, through the opening into his observatory, he noticed that it was unusually light out of doors, and that not only the ship, but the ice in the distance, was as plainly visible as if it had been full moonlight. No aurora, however, could be discerned through the thick clouds that covered the sky. It would appear then, that this unusual declination was in some way connected with the Northern Lights, though it was to be east and not the west, as usual.' Nansen's location at that time probably would have put the compass on an angle of forty-five degrees, if not more. Unless the needle was suspended on a thread, where it could move independently, it might assume any position but the right one. What influence makes the compass assume a vertical position? (Transcriber's note: The answer, of course, is that after one enters the opening at the Pole and travels _down_ instead of horizontally on the earth's surface, and is in "the land beyond the Pole", the needle must necessarily point up, toward the north magnetic pole, rather than north, as it did when one was traveling on the earth's horizontal surface.)

Chapter IV. "AROUND THE CURVE". "In passing round the curve leading into the interior of the earth, it seems difficult for some people to understand how water can be made to stay on the edge of the earth. Whether gravity is something in the earth that draws, or something in the air that repels, I do not know, nor do I know anyone that does. Gravity at the curve, or, at the turning into the interior of the earth, acts like a large magnet. Take a magnet, bent in a circular form, and see if there be any difference inside or outside. The experiment will show the attraction to be the same on either side. On page 396, Nansen again writes: 'Taking everything into calculation, if I am to be perfectly honest, I think this is a wretched state of matters. We are now in about 80 degrees north latitude; in September we were in 79 degrees; that is, let us say, one degree for five months. If we go on at this rate we shall be at the Pole in forty-five, or say fifty months, and in ninety or a hundred months at 80 degrees north latitude on the other side of it (the Pole), with probably some prospect of getting out of the ice and home in a month or two more. At best, if things go on as they are doing now, we shall be home in eight years.

"Whenever the explorers pass into the interior of the earth, as they have been passing, they meet such different situations that all are puzzled to account for what, under conditions expected, would be plain and simple. This shows that there is something going on entirely foreign to the ordinary fixed rules of the universe as man understands them; therefore no wonder they call it the strange land. Everyone that has spent considerable time in the Arctic or Antarctic circles has met with conditions unexplainable when based on the theory that the earth is round - each one easily accounted for, however, when treated on what now seems a fixed fact, that the earth is hollow.

"Greely's description on page 265 of passing round the curve of the earth is exceedingly good and clear; 'The deep interest with which we had hitherto pursued our journey was now greatly intensified. The eye of civilized man had not seen, nor his feet trodden, the ground over which we were traveling. A strong, earnest desire to press forward at our best gait seized us all. As we neared each projecting spur of the high headlands, our eagerness to see what was beyond became so intense at times as to be painful. Each point we reached, and a new landscape in sight, we found our pleasure not unalloyed, for ever in advance was yet a point which cut off a portion of the horizon and caused a certain disappointment.

"If Greely and his companions were entering into the interior of the earth, they would certainly find that the earth has a greater curve near the Poles than at any other place; and as they passed over and around the farthest point north, each projection reached would be followed by another which always seemed to take in a part of the horizon. This is just what they experienced."

Chapter IX. "ROCK, DUST POLLEN ON ICE." "When it can be shown that the conditions are such that no Arctic icebergs can be formed on earth, then they must be formed in the interior. If the material that produces colored snow is a vegetable matter (which the analysis shows), and is supposed to be a blossom or the pollen of a plant, when none such grows in the vicinity of the Arctic Ocean, then it must grow in the interior of the earth; for if it grew elsewhere on earth, then the snow would be colored in other locations as well, which does not seem to be the case. The dust, so annoying in the Arctic Ocean, is also produced by volcanic eruptions. Being light, it is carried far away by the wind, and when it falls on the ships it is disagreeable. When it falls with the snow, it produces black snow, and when analyzed, is found to consist of carbon and iron - supposed to come from some burning volcano. Where is that volcano? No record or account of any near the North Pole is found, and if it be anywhere else, why does the dust fall in the Arctic Ocean?

"Various explorers report large rocks and boulders on and

imbedded in the icebergs. These boulders are either cast there by the exploding volcano, or they are scraped up as the bergs slide down the rivers in the Inner Earth. The dust in the Arctic is so heavy that it floats in great clouds. It colors the snow black; it falls on the ships in such great abundance that it is a source of irritation. Nansen declares that it was one of his principal reasons for wanting to go home. If the earth is solid, there is no answer to this perplexing problem. But if the earth be hollow, the eruption of volcanoes on the interior easily can account for this dust."

Chapter XI. "OPEN WATER AT FARTHEST POINT NORTH". "It is claimed by many that the Arctic Ocean is a frozen body of water. Although it always contains large bodies of drift-ice and icebergs, it is not frozen over. The student of Arctic travels will invariably find that explorers were turned back by open water, and many instances are cited where they came near being carried out to sea and lost. What I wish to present to the reader, however, is the proof that the Arctic Ocean is an open body of water, abounding with game of all kinds, and the farther one advances, the warmer it will be found. There are many cases of clouds of dust or smoke. Many fogs are reported in winter time. If the earth were solid, and the ocean extended to the Pole, or connected with land surrounding the Pole, there would be nothing to produce that fog. It was caused by the warm air coming from the interior of the earth. On page 236, Kane says: 'Indeed, some circumstances which he (McGary) reports seem to point to the existence of a north water all the year round; and the frequent water-skies, fogs, etc., that we have seen to the S.W. during the winter, go to confirm the fact.'

"There are many pages of reports of this open sea to the far north. Greely speaks of open water the year round. If there be open water the year round at the farthest point north, can any good reason be assigned why all have failed to reach the Pole? The men that have spent their time, comfort and, in several cases, their lives, were all men more than anxious to succeed, yet, strange to say, all failed. Was this because the weather got warmer, and they found the game more plentiful? No, it was because there was no such place.

"Those islands -- passed during the long drift and travel for over a year - were undoubtedly islands that had never been seen before. It is more than likely that Nansen and his crew were farther into the interior than anyone had previously been. If they for one moment could have understood that the earth was hollow, conditions that seemed unexplainable and unaccountable would have been perfectly clear; but as they never dreamed of that, it is not strange that they are constantly mixed, and that currents and winds were always going and coming contrary to customs and theories.

"If Nansen was not sailing north, where was he sailing? He ought to have covered a long distance, as he speaks of making nine knots an hour. Had he only made five knots, the distance would have been nearly 2,000 miles, yet when he took his reckoning he found himself in latitude 79 degrees. If he had been going straight north, as he supposed he was, his sailing would have taken him over 12,000 miles past the Pole. Allowing for loss of speed, owing to the strength of the currents, and dodging bergs and floes, he would still have been beyond the Pole. This is the strongest proof possible that the earth is hollow, and that there is no way of reaching the spot where the North Pole is supposed to be. It is apparent that he went a long way into the interior of the earth.

"On page 229 he tells of losing sight of land entirely. 'In the course of the day we quite lost sight of land, and, strangely enough, did not see it again; nor did we see the islands of St. Peter and St. Paul, though, according to the maps, our course lay past them.' This statement shows that the explorer and his men knew nothing about where they were. If the charts showed that the islands mentioned above were on the ship's course, they were wrong, or Nansen did not know where he was.

"The reader will note what he says in regard to their location, 'and are always considerably west of our reckoning.' So far as knowing their exact position, they were, in fact, lost.

"On page 228, he remarks that it was a strange feeling to be sailing away north in the dark night to unknown lands, over an open, rolling sea, where no ship or boat had ever been before. 'We might have been hundreds of miles away in more southerly waters, for the air was so mild for September in this latitude.' They were surely in the interior of the earth at that point.

"Under date of Sept. 19th (the following day) he writes: 'I have never had such a splendid sail. On the north, steadily north, with a good wind, as fast as steam and sail can take us, and open sea mile after mile, watch after watch, through these unknown regions, always clearer and clearer of ice, one might almost say, 'How long will this last? The eye always turns to the northward as one paces the bridge. It is gazing into the future. But there is always the same dark sky ahead, which means open sea.'

"The reader will notice that the appearance of the sky shows the condition of the surface of the earth. This is due to the mirror sky, a phenomenon of the far north not fully explained even today, but may be due to ice particles high in the sky acting like a mirror and showing all explorers the conditions for many miles in all directions around them.

"In regard to their good fortune in finding clear sailing direct, as they supposed, toward the Pole, Nansen remarks; 'Henrick-sen answered from the crow's nest when I called up to him, 'They little think at home in Norway just now that we are sailing straight for the Pole in clear water.' No, they don't believe we have got so far. And I shouldn't have believed it myself if anyone had prophesied it to be a fortnight ago; but it is true.'

"He regards it as such good fortune that he asks himself, 'Is it not a dream?' Yet they were no nearer the Pole than they were two weeks before.

"He notes the phosphorescent water and the fish that looked like glowing embers. He saw an auk and later a sea-gull. Three weeks later he mentions that the water was still open. 'Afar as eye could see from the crow's nest with the small field glass, there was no end to the open water.'

14

"What puzzled him was the fact that after he had sailed from September 6th to 21st, with hardly any interruption, there was so much southerly current and no ice. That would lead to the impression there was no ice to the north, or it would have drifted with the south-going current, and closed the vast body of open water he had sailed through. It is evident that the ice in the Arctic is confined to the floes that come from the interior of the earth. Another evidence that he had advanced far into the interior of the earth is the quantity of fresh water he met.

"After all the foregoing evidence, is it possible that anyone can believe that the respective oceans are frozen bodies of water? If they do not believe that these oceans are frozen, why do the explorers fail to reach the Poles - if there be such places?"

Chapter XII. "WHY IT IS WARMER NEAR THE POLES." One of the principal proofs that the earth is hollow is that it is warmer near the Poles. If it can be shown by quoting those who made the farthest advance toward the supposed Poles, that it is warmer, that vegetation shows more life, that game is more plentiful than farther south, then we have a reasonable right to claim that the heat comes from the interior of the earth, as that seems to be the only place from which it could come.

"In 'Captain Hall's Last Trip', page 166, we read: 'We find this a much warmer country than we expected...bare of snow and ice... We have found that the country abounds with life, and seals, game, greese, ducks, musk-cattle, rabbits, wolves, foxes, bears, partridges, lemmings, etc.'

"Nansen draws special attention to the warmth and says, 'We might almost imagine ourselves at home.' This was at one of the farthest points north reached by anyone, and yet the weather was mild and pleasant.

"It will be observed that these extremely strong winds from the interior of the earth not only raise the temperature considerably in the vicinity of the Arctic Ocean, but affect it very materially four hundred and fifty miles away. Nothing could raise the temperature in such a manner, except a storm coming from the interior of the earth.

"Greely states: 'Surely this presence of birds and flowers and beasts was a greeting on nature's part to our new home.' Does that sound as if he had expected to find these things there, or that their presence was an everyday occurence? No. It was written in a tone of surprise. From what place had these birds and game come? South of them for many miles the earth is covered with a perpetual snow - in many locations, thousands of feet deep. They are found in that location in summer; and as it is warmer farther north, they would not be likely to go to a colder climate in winter. They seem to pass into the interior of the earth, as far as suits their nature. Let me state that the mutton-birds of Australia leave that continent in September, and no one has ever been able to find out where they go. My theory is that they pass into the interior of the earth, via the South Pole. (Transcriber's note: It is, however, a question whether the earth's south polar opening is open as is the one at the North Pole, or covered by several miles of ice of the frozen continent of Antarctica. The comparative absence of animal life at the South Pole, where penquins are the only inhabitants, might indicate that the entrance there is closed by ice.)

Where could one go and find such an abundance of game as at the farthest point north reached? The game is found there in summer. Can anyone tell where it goes in winter? Greenland is covered with snow from one to ten thousand feet deep. If the game is found at the extreme northerly points in summer, is it reasonable to suppose it would migrate to a colder climate in winter? It would be better to stay where it is. Greely tells us that the trails indicate that the musk-oxen make their winter quarters there. Since it becomes warmer as they go north, instinct tells them not to go south in winter. And if they do not go south, they must go into the interior of the earth. Nansen says (Vol. II, page 75): 'I cannot help believing that a land which, even in April, teems with bears, auks and black guillemots, and where seals are basking on the ice, must be a Canaan, flowing with milk and honey.' I am quite sure that the game passes into the interior of the earth, as many of the birds are heavy, and not built for short journeys. Schwatka saw a flock of four million auks - they darken the sky.

Chapter XV. "WHAT PRODUCES COLORED SNOW IN THE ARCTIC?" Why is the snow colored in the Arctic regions? The snow has been analyzed, and the red, green and yellow have been found to contain vegetable matter, presumably a flower, or the pollen of a plant. The black snow has also been analyzed, and found to contain carbon and iron, supposed to come from a volcanic eruption. But whence did they come? A flower that produced pollen sufficient to permeate the air with such density that it colored the snow, would require a vast territory - millions of acres - to grow it. Where is that to be found? It must be near the North Pole, for, if it grew elsewhere, colored snow would be found at other locations, and not be confined to the Arctic regions. As no such flowering plant is known on earth, we must look elsewhere.

"The interior of the earth is the only spot that will furnish us with an answer to the question. As the colors fall at different seasons, it is fair to presume that the flower matures at those seasons. It is also easy to find out where the black snow, frequently mentioned by the explorers, comes from. It comes out of an exploding volcano - of the kind that covered Nansen's ship with dust. All unexplained questions could be easily answered if one would believe that the earth is hollow. It is impossible to answer them under any other theory.

"Kane, in his first volume, page 44, says: 'We passed the Crimson Cliffs at Sir John Ross in the forenoon of August 5th. The patches of red snow from which they derive their name could be seen clearly at the distance of ten miles from the coast. It had a fine deep rose hue, not at all like the brown stain which I noticed when I was here before. All the gorges and ravines in which the snow had lodged were deeply tainted with it. I had no difficulty in justifying the somewhat poetical nomenclature which Sir John Franklin applied to this locality, for if the snowy surface were more diffused, as it is no doubt earlier in the season, crimson would be the prevailing color.'

"Kane speaks of the red snow as if it had a regular season in which to appear - as he says, 'if the snowy surface were more diffused as it is no doubt earlier in the season.' In another place he speaks of the red snow being two weeks later than usual. Now taking the fact into account that the material that colors the snow is a vegetable matter, supposed to be the blossom or pollen of a plant, and that no such plant grows on earth, where does it come from. The time for its appearance must grow on the interior of the earth.

Chapter XVI. "WHERE AND HOW ARE ICEBERGS FORMED?" As already stated, it is impossible for an iceberg to form at any place where it is warmest at the mouth of the stream or canyon. If it be warmer at the mouth than farther inland, the mouth would be the last to freeze over, and there would be no water to pass over the ice to make an iceberg. If one was formed - it being warmer at the mouth - it would commence to thaw there first, and where would water come from to break it loose and push it into the ocean? It could not start until the whole length of the river was thawed loose, and would then have to come down as a whole, as there would be nothing to break it. It is simply out of the question for an iceberg to form in any location yet discovered. On the other hand, the interior of the earth - back from the mouth of rivers or canyons - being warmer, is just suited for the formation of icebergs. The mouth freezes first, and the river, continuing to flow to the ocean, overflows the mouth, and freezes for months, until spring. As the warm weather of summer advances, and, owing to the warmth of the earth, the bergs are thawed loose, the water from the rains in the interior rushes down, and they are shoved into the ocean, and tidal waves are started.

"Note the difference. On the outer earth, the whole length of a stream is frozen, and the farther inland the harder the freezing, while in the interior of the earth, only the mouth is frozen, and the open water is well supplied with rains to produce bergs. In the interior of the earth, also, there is not only plenty of water to produce bergs, but plenty to shove them into the ocean, while on the outer earth there isn't water for either purposes.

"For the last three hundred years a fairly steady stream of explorers have been trying to reach the Poles - Arctic and Antarctic - and no one has ever seen an iceberg leaving its original location, and plunging into the ocean. Isn't it strange that no one has thought of asking about the place of their origin?

"What is to be found in the Antarctic Ocean to bear out the theory that icebergs come from the interior of the earth, and cannot be formed on earth? Bernacchi says: "Bernechi says: 'There was less than two inches of rainfall in eleven and one-half months, and while it snowed quite frequently, it never fell to any great depth. Under these conditions, where would materials be found to produce an iceberg? Yet the greatest one on earth is there - one so large that it is called the Great Ice Barrier, rather than an iceberg - being over four hundred miles long and fifty miles wide. It is grounded in two thousand one hundred feet of water, and extends from eighty to two hundred feet above water.

"Now it would be impossible for this berg to form in a country having practically no rain or snow. As icebergs are made from frozen water, and there is no water to freeze, it evidently was formed at

same place other than where it now is. The berg itself, being of
<u>fresh</u> water, lies in mid-ocean of salt water. (Transcriber's note:
How could an iceberg be formed of fresh water in the midst of a sea
of salt water? Where did the fresh water come from? It could not
come from a salt water sea. The only explanation is that the fresh
water came from rivers from the interior of the earth that flowed
toward the Arctic Sea, and when they reached there, the lower temperature caused them to freeze, and as more water poured over the
frozen part, it froze too, and so icebergs were built up, until
finally the flowing waters of the river pushed them into the sea.)

        "How do I know that the great ice barrier came from the interior
of the earth, and from the kind of river described? First, it could
not come from the exterior of the earth, as bergs are not formed there.
That river must have been 2,500 feet deep, fifty miles across and
from four to five hundred miles long; for those are the present
dimensions of the berg. The river had to be straight or the berg
could not have passed out without breaking. It passed through a comparatively level country for the surface is still flat. Another
proof that the interior of the earth is level near the Antarctic
entrance is that many of the icebergs found in the Antarctic are long
and slim. They are called 'ice tongues', which indicates that they
came out of rivers running nearly on a level. The bergs found in the
Arctic, on the other hand, are more chunky, indicating that they come
from a more mountainous country, where the fall of streams is more
abrupt, causing the bergs to be shorter and probably thicker.

        "When Bernacchi was voyaging in the Antarctic, he wrote: "During
the next two days we passed some thousands of icebergs, as many as
ninety being counted from the bridge at one time. There was very
little variety of form among them, all being very large and bounded
by perpendicular cliffs. There was a large quantity of fresh water
at the surface, derived from the number of icebergs.'

        "How does this account accord with your notion of how icebergs
are formed in a country where Bernacchi reports less than two inches
of rainfall in a whole year, and but small quantities of snow? Where
is the water to come from that will produce such great quantities of
icebergs averaging a thousand feet in thickness, and many of them
several miles long? Those icebergs were on their way north - never
to return - yet the ocean will always be filled with them, as others
will come from the place where they came. Where is that place?
There is no rain or melted snow to furnish the water to freeze into
an iceberg. Bergs can come from one place only - the <u>interior</u> of the
earth.

        Chapter XVII. "THE TIDAL WAVE" The writer here repeats many
descriptions of tidal waves by various explorers. They go right
through the great ice fields and lift the ice to great heights and
can be heard for miles in the distance before they reach the ship
and for miles after they pass beyond the ship. 'Giant blocks pitched
and rolled as though controlled by invisible hands, and the vast
compressing bodies shrieked a shrill and horrible song that curdled
the blood. On came the frozen waves. Seams ran and rattled across
them with a thundering boom, while silent and awestruck we watched
their terrible progress.' They were caused by some tremendous
agency and I can think of nothing more powerful than the plunging
of an iceberg into the ocean. The great frequency of these powerful
tidal waves seems to exclude the possibility of their being caused

by underwater volcanic eruptions."

A REVIEW OF THE BOOK, "A JOURNEY TO THE EARTH'S INTERIOR,
OR HAVE THE POLES REALLY BEEN DISCOVERED?"
BY MARSHALL B. GARDNER
PUBLISHED AT AURORA, ILLINOIS IN 1920

We must thank Mr. Ottmar Kaub for the above condensation of
Reed's book and for the following summary of Gardner's work on the
same subject which appeared fourteen years later. Reed's book was
published in London in 1906, while Gardner's was published in Illinois.
It seems that these two men reached the same conclusions independently,
and this independence of deduction is borne out by the fact that,
although Gardner lists about 50 books in his bibliography, he does
not list the book by Reed, nor make mention of Reed, nor does either
Reed or Gardener refer to any other investigator who arrived at the
same conclusions as himself. Kaub writes:

"The photographs of these two men show strength of body and of
character. They are rugged, independent thinkers, men who arrive at
their conclusions only after studying all the available facts and
then fearlessly declaring the logical result. Under the photo of
Gardner are the words: "Author of the theory of a central sun within
the Earth's interior."

"Neither author tells anything of his own vocation nor how he
became interested in this subject, or who paid for the cost of publishing their respective books. Perhaps an investigation will dis-
close some valuable facts about these two men. Have there been any
other people who reached the same conclusions as Reed and Gardner, but
who never put their beliefs in the form of a book or article? What
have been the true opinions of modern explorers such as Amundson,
Shakelton and Admiral Byrd? And, what is most important, what have
recent explorers found - and concealed? Is there a well kept secret -
and if so, why? What is the reason for the race of twelve nations
to Antarctica? Why are submarines going to the north and claim to
have traversed the geographical pole under the ice? Are flying
saucers coming from the interior of the Earth, as claimed by some
writers? Have any surface inhabitants been taken to the Earth's
interior on flying saucers? If so, who are they? Will they con-
tribute confirmation, based on actual observation, of the conclusions
of Reed and Gardner concerning the Earth having a hollow interior?
And a host of questions will arise if the interior is inhabited, as
some claim. Time may supply the answers."

Gardner's book is 450 pages in length. With fifty books in his
bibliography, he was most thorough in his research. Gardner claimed
that the Earth is a hollow shell approximately 800 miles thick in its
crust, with an opening at each polar end of approximately 1,400 miles
across. He says that the mammouth still lives in the interior, which
is its true origin. He points out that birds and animals migrate
to the north to find warmer weather in which to feed and breed. As
explorers go north of 80 degrees north latitude, they find the water
becoming warmer due to a warm current coming from the polar region.

19

They find red pollen on the icebergs and glaciers. And they find logs and other debris washed down in these warm currents.

Gardner writes: "That the musk-ox is not the only animal to be found where we should hardly expect it, is evident from another note in Hayes' diary. When he was in latitude 78 degrees, 17 minutes, early in July, he says: 'I secured a yellow-winged butterfly, and - who would believe it - a mosquito. And these I add to ten moths, three spiders, two bumble bees and two flies.'

In many pages of evidence Gardner discusses the bright lights seen shining from the polar caps of Mars, Venus and Mercury, and deduces that these planets all have central suns shining through their polar openings. He claims that the earth has the same and that the Aurora Borealis results from the projection of the rays of the central sun, passing through the North Polar opening, on the night sky.

Gardner cites the valuable observations made by Greely, who, in 1881, began his "Three Years of Arctic Service", as he called his book.

In the preface to this book, Greely tells us that the wonders of the Arctic regions are so great that he modified his actual notes made at the time, and understated them rather than lay himself open to the suspicion of exaggerating. That the Arctic regions are so full of life and strange evidence of a life farther north, that an explorer cannot describe it all without being accused of exaggerating, is surely a very strange thing if those regions only lead to a barren Pole of everlasting ice.

Greely reports birds of an unknown species, butterflies, flies and temperatures of 47 to 50 degrees and plenty of willow to make fires, also much fresh driftwood. He found two flowers different from any that he had ever seen.

Gardner states that he spent twenty years in research before publishing his book. Gardner's greatest contribution is that of the central sun, which he proves conclusively is the source of the aurora and of the possibility of plant and animal life in the earth's interior - and human life as well. As indicated above, Gardner claims that all planets are hollow and possess central suns. As a result of centrifual force, their rotation during their early formation when yet molten, caused their heavier constituents to be thrown toward their outer surface to form a crust, leaving the interior hollow, while a portion of the original fire remained there to form a central sun, also, the force of their rotation and movements through space caused openings to form at their polar extremities.

Mr. Ottmar Kaub, Dr. Marlo's secretary, who has had access to surviving rare copies of Reed's and Gardner's books, both of which mysteriously disappeared and became unknown to the world, whose excellent compilation of their data made possible the above summary, says that since both Reed and Gardner used the same source materials, which is the reports of Arctic explorers, and since both came to the same conclusions, there is no need to burden the reader by repeating what has already been said in reference to Reed's book. Kaub hopes that those who have visited the interior of the Earth by means of flying saucers and observed the central sun, which Gardner never saw, because he was never there, and who conversed with advanced scientists there who are the creators of the flying saucers, will verify Reed's and Gardner's theories. Dr. George Marlo, director of the UFO World Research Organization, whose secretary Mr. Kaub is, has done just that. We will consider his experiences in later pages.

Why have Reed's and Gardner's books become so rare that it is practically impossible to obtain a copy, it being by the rarest good fortune that Mr. Kaub found copies of each book which he read and which provided the basis for the above report? Because there exists a land area not recorded on any map, which is nearly equal to, or perhaps greater, than the entire land area of the Earth's surface - this uncharted land area being on the inside of the Earth's crust in its hollow interior. Naturally any government that learned about this vast territory would have ambitions to be the first to enter it and claim it, for which reason it would make every effort to keep this information secret, so that no other government might learn about it and claim this new territory first. This may explain the reason for the mysterious disappearance of Reed's and Gardner's books, and why, when Admiral Byrd, years later, flew by plane into the North Polar opening for 1700 miles into "the mysterious land beyond the Pole", which was not shown on any map, and saw mountains, forests, green vegetation, rivers, lakes and animals there, this remarkable discovery was hushed up and forgotten too. Dr. George Marlo writes:

"Marshall B. Gardner was right in 1920 when he wrote his book. On Aug. 3, 1894, Dr. Fritjof-Nansen was the first man in history to reach the Inner Earth. Dr. Nansen got lost and was big enough to admit it. He was surprised at the warm weather there. When he found a fox track, he knew it was lost.

"How could a fox track be here?", he wondered. That puzzled him. Had he known that he had entered the opening that leads to the hollow interior of the Earth and that this was the reason why, the further north he went the warmer it got, he would have found not only fox tracks but later tropical birds and other animals, and finally human inhabitants of this "land beyond the Pole", into which Admiral Byrd penetrated for 1700 miles by plane and which completely mystified him.

Theodore Fitch wrote a booklet, "Our Paradise Inside the Earth", based on the works of Reed and Gardner. He said that during the last century, a sea captain, who traveled due north, curved inward into the interior of the Earth, though he thought he was heading toward the North Pole. Fitch says that around the curve, inside the Earth, there is a ring of ice. Here the sea ended and they were blocked by an ice pack, which was very high, wide and deep. They could have landed and gone on further on foot, but no one ever did. Fitch believes that men could fly over these huge ice barriers, which was what Admiral Byrd did, when he penetrated by airplane for 1700 miles into this area not shown on any map.

Fitch writes: "Both William Reed and Marshall Gardner declare that there must be a land of paradise, with an ideal tropical climate, on the other side of the mammoth ice barrier. Both men are of the opinion that a race of little brown people live in the interior of the earth. It is possible that the Eskimos descended from these people. Reed's and Gardner's writings prove that the temperature on

21

the inside of the earth is more even than on the outside, being warmer in winter and cooler in summer. Also, there is much more rain, but it is never cold enough to snow. They claim that the opening in the earth is much greater in the south than in the north. (Author's note: This may be true but the absence of "Southern Lights" to correspond with Northern Lights, and the absence of the human and animal population of the Arctic region, would indicate that the South Polar opening must be covered by the ice of the frozen continent of Antarctica, which is many miles deep.)

"Most explorers have sailed straight north until they went around that 800 mile curve. Not one of them knew that they were on the inside of the earth. These explorers found things exactly opposite from what they expected. As they sailed north, the north wind became warmer and warmer. Except for strong, dusty, warm winds once in a while, the weather was mild and pleasant. Except for icebergs from the interior, the sea was open and the sailing good.

"They saw countless square miles of good land. The further north (really south) they went, the more grass, flowers, bushes, trees and other green vegetation they saw. One explorer wrote that his men gathered eight different kinds of flowers. Also that they saw sloping hills covered with green vegetation and more birds and animals than can be seen anywhere on earth.

"Another writer said they saw all kinds of warm weather animals and millions of tropical birds. They were so thick that a blind man could bring down one or more birds with one shot. The lovely scenery of both sky and land was more magnificent than anything ever seen on the exterior of the earth. Each explorer wrote about the majesty and grandeur of the aurora or Northern Lights. It is claimed that the Northern Lights really result from the light of the central sun inside the earth shining through the opening at the North Pole.

"William Reed says that the center of gravity is strongest about half way around the curve on the way to the interior of the earth. The gravitational pull there is so strong that the salt water and the fresh water from icebergs won't mix. The salt water remains a few feet below the fresh water. This enables one to obtain fresh drinking water from the Arctic Ocean.

"Around the curve, inside the earth, there is another ring of ice. It is called the great massive fresh water ice pack, or ice barrier. Each winter, this ring of ice is formed from fresh water flowing from inside the earth toward the outside. During the winter months, billions of tons of free-flowing fresh water coming from rivers flowing toward the outside of the earth through the opening that connects it with the inside freeze at their mouth. This causes mountains of ice. In the summer time, huge icebergs, miles long, break off and float to the outside of the earth, COMPOSED OF FRESH WATER, not of salt water. Where did this fresh water come from except from rivers of the inside of the earth? All water on the outside there is salty.

"Most writers on the subject claim that the interior of the earth is inhabited by a race of small brown-skinned people and also say that the Eskimos, whose racial origin differs from that of other races on the earth's surface, came from this subterranean race.

One explorer declared that those known as the Arctic Highlanders came
from the interior of the earth. When the Eskimos were asked where
their forefathers came from, they pointed to the north. Some Eskimo
legends tell of a paradisical land of great beauty to the north.
Eskimo legends tell of a beautiful land of perpetual light, where
there is neither darkness at any time nor a too bright sun. This
wonderful land had a mild climate, where large lakes never freeze,
where tropical animals roam in herds, and where birds of many colors
cloud the sky, a land of perpetual youth where people live for
thousands of years in peace and happiness. There is a story of a
British king called Herla, whom the Skraelings (Eskimos) took to a
land of paradise beneath the earth. The Irish have a legend about a
lovely land beyond the north where there is continuous light and
summer weather.

"The ancient writings of the Chinese, Egyptians, Hindus and
other races, and the legends of the Eskimos, speak of a great opening
in the north and a race that lives under the earth's crust, and that
their ancestors came from this paradisical land in the interior of
the earth.

"Gravitational pull is strongest around the curve from the
exterior to the interior of the earth. (Author's note: If the earth
has a hollow center, the center of gravity is not the geometrical
center of the earth, but the center of the solid crust, to which
inhabitants both above and below would adhere, and also it would
be greatest inside the opening between the outer and inner surface.)
A 150 pound man would probably weigh 300 pounds while sailing around
the curve. (Author's note: This is probably why airplane travel
is more difficult in this region and why no planes have yet reached
the earth's interior. It is claimed that only flying saucers can
make the trip successfully.) When he reached the inside of the
earth he would weigh only about 75 pounds. This is because less
force is needed to hold a body to the inside of a hollow ball, in
motion, than to hold it to the outside. (Author's note: This is
due to centrifugal force produced by rotation.)

"In these icebergs (that come out from the earth's interior)
the mammoth and other huge prehistoric tropical animals have been
found. These animals were frozen so suddenly with the coming of the
Ice Age that they still have green grass in their mouths and stomachs.
Tropical trees loaded with fruit have been found. Siberia and islands
of the north have great ivory deposits from huge mammals that lived
there when the climate was still tropical, before a shifting of the
earth on its axis suddenly turned it frigid."

Fitch asks those who do not believe that the earth is hollow in
its interior to answer the following questions:

"Can you produce proof that any explorer ever reached the so-
called north or south pole?

"If there is no such thing as 83 to 90 degrees latitude ON
earth, then how could one reach or fly over the North Pole?

"If the earth is not hollow, then why does the north wind in
the Arctic get warmer as one sails north beyond 70 degrees latitude?

"Why are there warm northerly winds and an open sea for hundreds of miles north of 82 degrees latitude?

"After 82 degrees latitude is reached, why is the needle of the compass always agitated, restless and balky?

"If the earth is not hollow, then why does that warm wind carry more dust than any wind on earth?

"If no rivers are flowing from the inside to the outside, then why are all icebergs composed of fresh water?

"Why does one find tropical seeds, plants and trees floating in the fresh water from these icebergs?

"If not all the fresh water icebergs positively do not come from any place ON earth, as would be impossible unless we assume the existence of rivers flowing from the inside to the outside, then where do they come from?

"If the inside of the earth is not warm, why do millions of tropical birds and animals go further north in the winter time?

"Why does the wind from the north carry more pollen and blossoms than any wind on the exterior?

"If it is not hollow and warm inside the earth, then why does colored pollen color the snow for thousands of square miles?

"Could it be that pollen from millions of acres and colored flowers causes the snow to be red, pink, yellow, blue, etc.?

Though his book was written in 1920, back in 1912, Marshall B. Gardener constructed a working model of the earth, according to his theory, which he later reproduced in his book as a diagram, below which appears the following explanation:

"Showing the earth bisected centrally through the polar openings and at right angles to the equator, giving a clear view of the central sun and the interior continents and oceans."

William L. Blessing published a booklet in which he reproduced the above diagram, as well as other diagrams in Gardner's and Reed's books, whose views be restated as follows:

"The earth is not a true sphere. It is flat at the poles, or I should say it begins to flatten out at the poles. The pole is simply the outer rim of a magnetic circle and at this point the magnetic needle of the compass points straight up. As the earth turns on its axis the motion is gyroscopic, like the spinning of a top. Let us say then that the outer gyroscope pole is the magnetic rim of a circle. Beyond the rim, the earth flattens and slopes gradually like a canyon into the earth's interior. The true pole in the exact center of the cone is perpendicular, for this point is the exact center of the opening or hollow into the earth's interior.

"There never has been a pole to pole trip made around the earth. The distance from pole to pole on the earth's surface is about

16,000 miles. The circumference from pole to pole would be 32,000 miles, while the circumference at the equator is exactly 24,899 miles.

"The total surface of the earth is 197 million square miles. The estimated weight is six sextillions of tons. If the earth had a solid core, the weight would be much greater, and if the earth were solid through and through, the ebb and flow of the tides would be impossible.

"The old idea that the earth was once a solid or molten mass and that at the center is still molten iron must be discarded. Since the shell of the earth is about 800 miles thick, that would mean that the molten iron core would be more than 7000 miles in diameter and 21,000 miles in circumference. Impossible!

"Likewise, the old idea that the deeper into the earth the hotter it becomes must also be discarded. It is radium and radioactivity that produces the heat in the earth. All surface rocks contain minute particles of radium. (Author's note: As against the belief that the deeper we go in the earth the hotter it becomes, so that its center is a fiery mass, it is more probable that heat increases until we reach the level of greatest radioactivity, where volcanic lava forms, which is the level of intensest heat, after passing which, heat progressively diminishes the deeper down we go, until we reach the earth's hollow interior.)

The following interesting facts support the idea of the earth having a hollow interior with openings at the Poles:

1.   Since the North Pole is warmer than the South Pole, the former being covered with ocean and comparatively less ice, which is steadily melting and diminishing, whereas the South Pole is covered by the frozen continent of Antarctica, with ice two miles deep and steadily increasing in amount, these facts, like the occurrence of Northern Lights without there being "Southern Lights", may be explained by the North Polar opening being free and permitting the passage of the rays of the central sun to heat this area, while in the case of the South Pole, lower temperatures that prevail there, with resulting blocking of the opening by ice, accounts for this difference and also for non-occurrence at the South Pole of seals, polar bears and other animals that came from the earth's interior, as well as Eskimos, who also are supposed to have had such an origin.

2.   The phenomenon of ocean waves and their steady ebb and flow, is explained by a circulation of ocean water through the polar openings, passing from the outer to the inner surface and vise versa, their rocking, undulating motion being produced by the combination of this circulation and the earth's various motions. While lunar magnetism may explain tides, it does not account for the constant back-and-forth rocking of ocean water.

3.   It is interesting to note that while there is soil found in the North Polar area, in the Antarctic there is only ocean water and ice. The lower temperature of the South Pole has caused a steady accumulation of ice, whereas the higher temperature at the North Pole has melted the ice and left bare land visible. It is probable that at the South Pole, ice has blocked up the opening.

The writer believes that the truest conception of the structure of the earth must be based on the idea that in its early formation, perhaps at a much greater speed of rotation, when still in a liquid, molten state, centrifugal force caused the heavy substances in its interior - rocks and metals - to be thrown toward the outer periphery, forming a solid crust about 800 miles thick and leaving the interior portion hollow, with openings at the poles, while some of the original fire remained to form the central sun.

From the evidence on hand we must come to the following conclusions, confirmed by Arctic exploration:

1. There is really no North or South Pole. Where the Poles are supposed to exist there are really openings to the hollow interior of the Earth.

2. Most flying saucers come from an opening beyond the North Pole, that is, from the hollow interior of the earth. It is claimed that the direction of flight of saucers is mostly north and south for this reason, since they come out and return back to a polar opening.

3. The hollow interior of the Earth enjoys an ideal subtropical climate of about 76 degrees in temperature.

4. The so-called "Island in the Sky", seen after one enters the polar opening, is a reflection of the Earth's surface on the sky, which acts as a mirror, a phenomenon characteristic of the trans-Arctic region, which was observed by many explorers. This "Island in the Sky" is probably what Admiral Byrd referred to when he used the expression, "enchanted continent in the sky". The meaning of this strange expression may be interpreted as follows. After you leave the polar area and enter into the North Polar opening, what first strikes you is the Aurora Borealis, formed by the projection of the light of the inner sun on the night sky of the Arctic region. You also see the "Island in the Sky" or the "Water-Sky", which is a reflection of land below the sky, creating an optical illusion of an island in the sky.

5. There is an outblowing of dust from the interior of the Earth, coming from active volcanos inside the polar opening. This dust greatly disturbed Arctic explorers and discolored the snow and ice on which it settled. How there could be dust in this region, and more dust the further north one traveled, could have no other explanation.

6. It is claimed that the central sun, being smaller than our sun, is dimmer, even though nearer, and looks blood red sometimes.

7. The existence of a polar opening and land beyond the Pole is a Government top secret, since the major nations are now secretly seeking an entrance into the interior of the Earth through the North Polar opening. The big problem is how to get there alive.

8. There is a large population inside the Earth, which composes a civilization far in advance of our own, as shown by the fact that they use flying saucers for transportation. It is claimed that the hollow interior of the Earth is a true paradise.

9. Icebergs come from the interior of the Earth. Since they are composed of fresh water they must be formed from rivers coming from the interior and reaching the surface through the polar opening, freezing into ice as they pass from the warm temperature inside to the cold region on the outside of the Earth.

10. It is from the warm interior of the Earth that the progenitors of seals, polar bears, walrusses, mammoths and other Arctic animals originally came. The ancestors of the Eskimos also came from this "mysterious land beyond the Pole", according to their legends and traditions. Since there are no Eskimos, seals or polar bears in the Antarctic region we must conclude that the opening there is more difficult of passage and the temperature lower, as evidenced by the heavier ice formation there as compared to the Arctic.

ADMIRAL BYRD CONFIRMS REED'S AND GARDNER'S THEORY OF A NORTH POLAR OPENING

In February 1947, Admiral Richard E. Byrd took off from an Arctic base and flew north to the Pole. He then kept flying north beyond the Pole and was surprised to discover iceless lands, lakes, mountains covered with trees and even a monstrous animal moving through the underbrush below! For almost 1700 miles the plane flew over land, mountains, trees, lakes, rivers. After flying 1700 miles he was forced to turn back because of his gasoline supply limit for the return trip. He returned to his Arctic base.

Not much was thought about this unusual observation at the time and the matter was forgotten until December 1959, when Ray Palmer, in the issue of his magazine "FLYING SAUCERS - THE MAGAZINE OF SPACE CONQUEST", called the world's attention to Byrd's sensational report, which he interpreted to indicate that Byrd had actually entered into the North Polar opening leading to the hollow interior of the earth, which was the place, Palmer concluded, where flying saucers originate.

Following the appearance of Palmer's magazine, the other outstanding authority on flying saucers, Gray Barker, editor of "THE SAUCERIAN BULLETIN", in his January 15, 1960 issue, seems to have become convinced also. Commenting on Palmer's report on Byrd's observations, Barker writes:

"According to Byrd's reported flight, he shouldn't have seen anything but ice-covered ocean or partially-open water. Yet Byrd saw trees and other greenery. According to the globe, such a land just isn't there.

"Palmer next discusses similar geographical discrepancies at the South Pole, then draws an amazing conclusion:

"THE EARTH IS NOT SPHERICAL : INSTEAD IT IS SOMETHING LIKE A DOUGHNUT, though perhaps not so flattened. At each pole there is a huge opening, so large that when one travels 'beyond' the pole, he actually enters the lip of the hole of the doughnut-shaped earth. If he traveled far enough he would travel through the 'hole' of the doughnut and emerge at the other Pole.

"PALMER FURTHER SUGGESTS THAT PEOPLE LIVE ON THE 'INSIDE' OF THE EARTH, that such people emerge from the poles in flying saucers!

"He promises to present the remainder of his proofs later, but in the present issue of FLYING SAUCERS his case boils down to these main points:

"(1) Measurements of areas at the North and South Poles are larger than you can find room for on a map or globe, leading to the assumption that such areas extend down into the 'doughnut'.

"(2) Some animals, particularly the musk-ox, migrate north in the wintertime, from the Arctic Circle. Foxes are found north of the 80th parallel, heading north, and appear well fed in a land where there is no food visible.

"(3) Arctic explorers agree it gets warmer as one heads north.

"(4) In the Arctic, coniferous trees drift ashore, from out of the north. Butterflies and bees are found in the far north. Butterflies and bees are found in far north, but never hundreds of miles south of that point.

"(5) Remains of mammoths, perfectly preserved, were found in Siberia, with the sparse food of the sub-Arctic region in its stomach. Such food could not have supported the animal. It must have come from 'the land beyond the Pole', Palmer postulates.

"(6) Trouble with satellites shot over the South Pole bears out either the theory that land areas haven't been measured accurately, or that 'somebody' has been interfering with them.

"Personally, the editor has never exactly made up his mind as to where the saucers came from. But he has always held a sneaking suspicion that when we ponder the origin of them, we somehow may be overlooking something - overlooking the obvious. I remember that the following idea has often come into my mind: 'What if there could be some unknown race, on some unexplored portion of the earth, which is responsible for the saucers? Palmer's article started me to thinking along that direction once again.

"THE INNER EARTH EXPLANATION WOULD FIT INTO MOST, IF NOT ALL THE FACETS OF THE SAUCER PICTURE.

"Let us accept, for a moment, that such a people had existed inside the earth for thousands of years, even before man - or perhaps they seeded the outside with man. Maybe they have constantly watched over him and guided him, occasionally sending great teachers among him, occasionally assisting him with technology, giving rise to what we now call 'legends'. Maybe they built the great pyramid; may be they are responsible for some of the 'miracles' reported in secular and religious histories.

"Such people would probably possess the means to travel into space, to hold commerce with peoples on other planets, even outside our solar system. Until man, their protege, learned to be morally worthy, they would not wish to give him, suddenly, the knowledge of their existence or secrets of their technology.

"When man, however, invented the atomic bomb, the people of the inner earth would be greatly concerned about it. Maybe they would fear contamination which could reach them; maybe they would fear man could blow up the earth entirely; maybe they would be concerned only with man's own welfare.

"Halting or controlling man's propensity for destruction would be a delicate problem, unless they would come out openly and inform him of their existence. Maybe they would figure they would eventually have to do so, and began a slow process of indoctrination, first merely letting him see the saucers flying around. When they learned man thought the saucers were from space, they would pretend to be space people 'contacting' him in their craft and trying to indoctrinate him with peaceful philosophy (the reader will remember that the majority of 'space people' have spoken out strongly against the Bomb)".

After agreeing with Ray Palmer that the theory that the saucers come from the hollow interior of the earth is much more reasonable than the interplanetary theory, Gray Barker refers to the "Antarctic Mystery", namely the appearance of "three men in black" who hushed several flying saucer editors who dared to announce the theory that saucers came from a base in the Antarctic. One of these was A. K. Bender. On this point Barker writes:

"Maybe people like Albert K. Bender have figured out the obvious, and the people of the inner earth have stopped him. It would indeed be frightening to face three men who could prove they were from the inside of the earth by being able to make some concrete demonstration of that fact.

"Those who have read my book ('They Knew Too Much About the Flying Saucers') will remember that before being 'slushed up', Bender, a New Zealand and an Australian saucer group were charting the paths of the saucers, with the idea of projecting lines and determining a point of origin or rendevous of the craft. Bender told Harold Fulton of Civilian Saucer Investigation he believed that saucers might be based in the Antarctic. F. Jarrold, of the Australian Flying Saucer Bureau, agreed with Bender, and suggested they start what they would term 'Project X', concerned with charting the paths of sightings. Right after that Bender clammed up, and Jarrold also complained of a strange visitor, and shortly thereafter abandoned saucer research."

The significance of this was that the subterranean people who sent the flying saucers up into our atmosphere to present its radioactive pollution to the extent of poisoning the air they must breathe, which eventually comes from the outer atmosphere through the polar opening, which was the reason for their mass visitation soon after the explosion of the first atomic bomb in Hiroshima, in order to keep up the illusion that they were "spacemen" who came from other planets and to preserve the secret of their true origin, i.e., the interior of the earth, silenced Bender and Jarrold lest they reveal this secret, which, at the time, they did not want surface people, who, in comparison with them, are "mechanized barbarians", to know.

Ray Palmer and Gray Barker, leading flying saucer experts in the United States, are therefore both convinced that saucers come from the interior of the earth and not from other planets as formerly supposed. But they did not originate this idea, which was born in Brazil many years before.

Professor Henrique de Souza, a Brazilian archeologist, esotericist and president of the Brazilian Theosophical Society, with headquarters at SaoLourenzo, in the state of Minas Gerais, Brazil, where the Society has built an immense temple of Greek style dedicated to "Agharta", Buddhist name of the Subterranean World, has many years ago claimed that flying saucers do not come from other planets but from the Subterranean World. Among the members of the Brazilian Theosophical Society who settled in Sao Lourenzo were Commander Paulo Strauss of the Brazilian Navy and O. C. Huguenin, a writer. Both were students of Professor de Souza.

Early in 1955, Commander Strauss delivered a series of lectures in Rio de Janeiro on the subject of the flying saucer in which he affirmed categorically that they were of terrestrial origin and did not come from other planets. He stated the startling conclusion that they came from the Subterranean World, the World of Agharta, as it is known among Buddhists and Theosophists. His lectures made such an impression that the most popular Brazilian magazine, "O Cruziero", published three articles on the 5th, 12th and 19 of February 1955, on his lectures, announcing to the world for the first time the theory that flying saucers had a subterranean origin.

Some time later, O. C. Huguenin published a book on this subject, which he dedicated to Professor de Souza, the originator of the idea, and starting off with a report of Commander Strauss lectures, entitled "FLYING SAUCERS:FROM THE SUBTERRANEAN WORLD TO THE SKY". In this book the author presents the astounding theory that flying saucers are really Atlantean aircraft, known as "Vimanas", which once flew in our atmosphere and which, prior to the destruction of Atlantis, were transferred to the Subterranean World, where they continued to fly in the earth's interior atmosphere, appearing only occasionally in the outer atmosphere, and more frequently in ancient times, when those whom they conveyed to visit us were considered as "gods". Huguenin writes:

"In the United States, George Adamski claimed to have been in contact with visitors in a flying saucer who claimed they came from Venus. This is apparently in contradiction to the statements of Commander Strauss (who maintained that flying saucers do not come from other planets but from the interior of the earth)." Huguenin then goes on to say that though the occupants of the flying saucer told Adamski they came from Venus, this was just a bluff, for they really came from the Subterranean World but had a special reason why they did not want to tell it to Adamski and so pretended that they came from Venus. And the same is true of other saucer contacts reported by other writers. In each case the saucers really came from the interior of the earth, but this fact was concealed and it was pretended that they came from other planets.

From the evidence on hand we must conclude that when people were taken on trips to Mars and other places on flying saucers, they really traveled to the interior of the earth, where exists an advanced civilization but were not told so, and instead were told they were in Mars. The reason for this secrecy is obvious. The subterranean people do not wish their existence known to surface "barbarians", or to power-mad militarists who might attempt an invasion with atomic weapons. For security reasons, it was to their advantage to maintain the bluff that they came from other planets. But since, according to Dr. Marlo, leading governments already know the secret, there is no longer any reason why it cannot be told to the public. However, the Government would rather that these important facts not be publicized, fearing that some other government might attempt the invasion before they do; and this explains the efforts of the Government to suppress all proof that flying saucers exist and its consistent policy of denying their existence. The reason for this is to conceal the secret of their true place or origin. By denying their existence, there would be less chance for their place of origin being found.

However, since the subterranean people have a civilization that is thousands of years in advance of our own in scientific development and command a form of energy far more powerful than atomic energy, the "vril" of Bulwer Lytton's "Coming Race", any attempted invasion must fail, since the subterranean people would defend themselves by projecting their Death Rays on the invaders which would disintegrate them into dissociated electrons, neutrons and protons, and cause them and their atomic weapons to disappear.

In his book, Huguenin claims that in February 1955, a flying saucer came to Sao Lourenzo, which was seen by many Theosophists who live there, and then men of great stature were seen to leave the apparatus and to salute Professor de Souza. He also quotes John Martins, in his articles in "O Cruziero", who stated that Professor de Souza had personally visited the Subterranean World. This was what he told the author when he visited him in 1957.

Huguenin points out that the behavior of the flying saucers does not fit into the theory that they are visitors from other planets. If they came from other planets, Huguenin says, they display "strange and incomprehensible conduct, when we consider how a terrestrial expedition traveling to Mars or any other planet would act. Certainly on reaching its destination, it would endeavor to establish cordial relations with its inhabitants. If so, why don't the pilots of flying saucers sent by Martians do the same, if they possess a grade of civilization more elevated than our own.

The answer to this question is that flying saucers came not for a mere "visit", but were sent by subterranean swellers in the hollow interior of the earth for the purpose of preventing further radioactive poisoning of our atmosphere, which would in turn poison the air they receive from outside. That this theory is correct, is indicated by the fact that the mass visitation of the saucers took place right after the Hiroshima atomic explosion and constituted an act of self-preservation. The subterranean theory also explains better than the interplanetary theory of the origin of the saucers why large fleets of saucers appeared in our sky following the Hiroshima explosion, their purpose being to attract our attention and convince us of the fact that a superior race came to visit us, in order to later convince us to suspend further atomic explosions so as not to contaminate the air they breathe, which comes from our atmosphere through the polar opening. This also explains why after their attempt to befriend us and convince governments of their existence failed, and after they were pursued by military planes rather than being cordially received, the previous fleets of saucers were withdrawn, and only isolated scouts remained in our atmosphere to conduct fallout measurements. Referring to the significance of the fact that this mass visitation took place only after the explosion of the first atomic bomb in Hiroshima and never before, Huguenin writes:

"If the flying saucers came from Mars - in spite of all the arguments we enumerated which disproved this to be possible - why don't their pilots enter into direct and frequent contact with humanity and why didn't they do it before, since they had thousands of years in which to do so?" And why did saucers from Mars and other planets all decide to visit us at the same time, though they had to travel different distances to reach us, would have been impossible if they all commenced their journey when the flash of the Hiroshima explosion reached them in 1945? Since this would be impossible, the only logical explanation is that they all came from the same place - the earth's interior atmosphere - coming out through the North Polar opening. Certainly the Hiroshima explosion of a small atomic bomb could not be a source of worry and danger to inhabitants of other planets millions of miles away, to cause them to come here in such great numbers so soon after the occurrence of this explosion, whereas if the saucers were sent by subterranean people, all these facts are more reasonably explained.

Another argument in favor of the subterranean theory and against the interplanetary theory of the origin of the saucers is the fact that if they came from other planets to visit us, they would have come and gone, and not have lingered for about fifteen years in our atmosphere, which they did. This is explained on basis of the conception that most of the saucers are scouts sent up by the subterranean people to conduct fallout measurements, so that subterranean scientists may be kept informed of the degree of radioactive poisoning of our atmosphere, so that they might adjust their air purifiers accordingly. On the other hand, if saucers came from other planets they would have no need to linger here so long or be so worried about our poisoning our atmosphere by our nuclear explosions, which could not affect them in any way.

Huguenin concludes his discussion with the following statement: "The hypothesis of the extre-terrestrial origin of the flying saucers does not seem acceptable". He claims they are of terrestrial origin; and since they did not come from any known nation, they came from an unknown race of people; also, since they did not come from any known part of the earth, they came from an unknown part of the earth- its _interior_. Thus, a few years before Ray Palmer and Gray Barker became convinced of the fact that flying saucers came from the subterranean world and not from other planets, as they did in 1959, Huguenin and Commander Strauss, in Brazil in 1955, held the same theory.

According to Huguenin, flying saucers were Atlantean aircraft which once flew in the outer atmosphere prior to the destruction of Atlantis, and since then continued to fly in the earth's interior atmosphere. While most of the Atlanteans perish when their continent sank under the Atlantic Ocean, a certain remnant of the race survived by gaining access to the Subterranean World, bringing their "vimanas" (flying saucers) with them. This occurred some 11,500 to 12,500 years ago.

Thus there exist on and in this planet two races, an inferior race of mortal men, who were short-lived, who inhabited the earth's surface, and a superior race of supermen, called "immortal gods" by the ancients, who inhabit the earth's interior. In ancient Pagan times they frequently contacted surface dwellers, and temples were built for their occupancy during their visits. But with the establishment of the Church of Rome, these temples were destroyed and the existence of the "gods of the underworld" was denied. Christian priests taught their followers that they were devils, evil beings who should be avoided, and that they should worship only an invisible god in the sky.

Thus the existence of a Subterranean World and its inhabitants became a lost memory. And just as religionists taught that it was an inferno of everlasting fire, so scientists preserved the error in their theory that the earth has a fiery core, basing this on the flimsy evidence that the furthur down one goes, the hotter it becomes Huguenin points out that the increase of temperature continues only until one reaches the level where volcanic lave originates, but after one passes this, it gets cooler and cooler until the hollow interior of the earth is reached.

After presenting the argument that flying saucers do not come from other planets nor from any existing nation on the earth surface, Huguenin concludes that they must come from the Subterranean World. He states his conclusion as follows:

"Finally, we must consider the most recent and interesting theory that has been offered to account for the origin of the flying saucers: the existence of a great Subterranean World with innumerable cities in which live millions of inhabitants...This other humanity must have reached a very high degree of civilization, economic organization and social, cultural and spiritual development, together with an extraordinary scientific progress, in comparison with whom the humanity that lives on the earth's surface may be considered as a race of barbarians.

"The idea of the existence of a Subterranean World will shock many people. To others it will sound absurd and impossible, for 'certainly', they would say, 'if it existed, it would have been discovered long ago.' And there are plenty of other critics who would point out that it would be impossible for such an inhabited world to exist inside the earth because of the belief that as one descends the temperature increases, on the basis of which theory it is supposed that, since the temperature increases the further down one goes, the center of the earth is a fiery mass. However, this increase in temperature does not mean that the center of the earth is fiery, since it might extend only for a limited distance and, as is the case with volcanoes and hot springs, arise from subterranean cavities located at certain levels (below which the temperature again drops as one goes downward)...In accordance with the hypothesis that heat increases as one descends through the earth's crust, this takes place only during a distance of eighty kilometers (in the superficial layer of the earth).

"According to the information supplied by Commander Paulo Justin Strauss, the Subterranean World is not restricted to caverns, but is more or less extensive and is located in a hollow inside the earth, large enough to contain cities and fields, where live human beings and animals, whose physical structure resembles those on the surface. Among its inhabitants are certain persons who came from the surface, who, like Colonel Fawcett and his son Jack, descended, never to return. (Huguenin here refers to the views of Commander Strauss and Professor de Souza on the controversial subject of Colonel Fawcett's mysterious disappearance, claiming that they are still alive in the Subterranean World, to which they gained access through a tunnel opening in the Roncador Mountains of northeast Matto Grosso, and were not killed by Indians as commonly supposed.)

Huguenin then asks how these marvelous subterranean cities and this advanced civilization in the earth's interior arose. He claims that its builders and most of its present inhabitants were and are members of antediluvian races that once inhabited the prehistoric polar continent of Hyperborea, the Pacific continent of Lemuria (which was submerged 25,000 years ago) and the Atlantic continent of Atlantis (which sank some 11,500 years ago). These are the race of gods or supermen, which are the master race of the Subterranean World. There is also a race of mortals, which came from the surface, composed mostly of Oriental yogis and Tibetan lamas, who gained entry as a result of a lifetime of striving and self-perfection through yoga practices. There are comparatively few Westerners there; and they are the great masters of past history, including such illustrious characters as Pythagoras, Apollonius of Tyana and Count Saint-Germain, whose deaths and brial places are unknown and who entered the Subterranean World after being last seen.

QUETZALCOATL, SUBTERRANEAN TEACHER WHO VISITED THE
AZTECS AND MAYAS ON A FLYING SAUCER

The name "Quetzalcoatl" means "winged serpent". The serpent symbolizes wisdom and a winged serpent represents a flying teacher who visited the Aztecs of Mexico and the Mayas of Yucatan and Central America on a flying saucer; and, after performing his mission, left and returned back to the Subterranean World from which he came. Quetzalcoatl was called God of the Wind, because he came through the air. He was described as "a man of good appearance and grave countenance, with white skin, a beard and dressed in a long flowing white garment". Obviously this tall white bearded subterranean Atlantean was a mere visitor among the short, brown-skinned, beardless Quiches and Mayas whom he came to teach and help, and not a member of their own race. However this teacher of vegetarianism, pacifism and chastity, who was called an Aztec Christ, made such a deep impression on these Indians, that he was not forgotten for centuries after he left them on the same flying saucer on which he arrived.

He was called by some Quetzalcoatl and by others Huemac, because of his great goodness. He taught the Indians the way of virtue by word and example. He forbade the killing of any living creature or the eating of carcasses (meat). He introduced among them the culti-vation of corn and recommended it as a basic food in the form of tortillas, which he taught them to make. These Indians owe their pacifistic traits to his influence, for he taught them to abstain from the use of arms. He hoped to save them from vice and gave them laws and a good doctrine to restrain them from their lewd and lustful ways, and he instituted fasting, vegetarianism and body hygiene among them. But seeing how little they followed this doctrine, he vanished, telling them that some day he would return.

When Cortez came to Mexico, one reason why he found it so easy to conquer the country was because the ruling monarch, Montezuma, believed that he was Quetzalcoatl, who returned. One reason why Montezuma feared Cortez and believed him to be Quetzalcoatl was because at the time of his arrival on the shore of Mexico a fireball gyrated over Mexico City. This was considered as an omen of the Return of Quetzalcoatl - on a flying saucer. However, it seems that at this time a flying saucer, that was mistaken for a comet, that threw forth sparks of fire, was seen to pass over the sky of Mexico, at which time the temple of the war god was seen to blaze without apparent cause. The priests tried to put the fire out, but the more water they poured on, the more it blazed. Then a lightning stroke hit the statue of the very war god. The big "comet" ran through the sky of Mexico, throwing off big sparks and leaving behind it a very long tail, while the lagoon of Mexico City (which was built on a lake) rose and boiled in fury, though there was no wind. The Spaniards took this to be a message from their God that he looked with favor upon their venture to obtain this great land for purposes of making ever greater numbers of Catholic converts. So while Cortez was not Quetzalcoatl, it seems some other Quetzalcoatl did return aboard a flying saucer, but did not land.

NEW LIGHT ON THE FAWCETT MYSTERY

When the writer went to visit Professor de Souza, the great Brazilian authority on the Subterranean World, he remarked that a few days ago he returned from one of his frequent visits to the Underworld, and that he had visited Shamballah, which is the capital city of Agharta (Buddhist name of the Subterranean World. Professor de Souza had been a student of Buddhism.)

The writer said he was anxious to visit the Subterranean World and asked Prof. de Souza to tell him where the entrance was. Since this is a great secret never told to an unknown person who did not prove he was worthy of trust that he would not reveal it to the unworthy, Prof. de Souza used the usual subterfuge by claiming it was in the Roncador Mountains where Fawcett was heading when last seen and where is supposed to exist the most famous opening of tunnels leading to the Subterranean World, which is guarded by fierce Chavantes Indians, who will kill anyone whom they suspected might molest their gods who dwell therein. Prof. de Souza gave the writer a password which he said would enable him to get through unharmed by the poisoned arrows of the Indians.

So the writer took a plane to Cuiaba, the last point where Fawcett left civilization some years past, heading straight northeast to Roncador, accompanied by his son Jack and Indian guides. In Cuiaba, chief city of central Matto Grosso, the writer met a missionary who said he was posted in the Chavantes territory through which Fawcett passed on his way to Roncador and that the Indians who killed him confessed the murder. But nothing was said about Jack being killed. In Cuiaba at the time was a white Indian who was supposed to be the son of Jack by an Indian mother.

While the above evidence that Fawcett was killed seems conclusive; there are those who believe he is still alive. On this subject, E. C. Fedrowisch, of LaCombe, La., writes:

"As reported in the New York Times, April 4, 1951, it is believed that the Great Fawcett Mystery is at it's end with his death at the hands of Kalopages Indians near the Rio dos Mortes (River of Death, on his way to Roncador) in Matto Grosso. Belongings of Fawcett were exhumed and the jaw bone believed to be Fawcett's was sent to his London dentist for identification. But no one in the papers said it was his.

"In 1925, Col. H. P. Fawcett, Jack and Raleigh Rimmel, Jack's friend, went into the jungles of Matto Grosso and disappeared. Everyone wanted to forget it, but it did not stop there.

"In May, 1930, Mrs. Nina Fawcett wrote a letter to Dr. Nandor Fodor, author of 'The Haunted Mind', and she said: 'Yesterday I received a most interesting communication - a very long letter indeed - from a lady in an out-of-the-way part of California - a stranger to me up till now - who I believe is half American Indian. Anyway she is in close touch with the Loas Pueblo Indians of New Mexico who are, as you probably know, masters of the science of telepathic communication. These Indians are very hurt at the imputation that 'the Fawcett party was killed by hostile Indians.' They say - and it is quite true - that Col. Fawcett made friends with the Indians long ago, and once having won their confidence and friendship, no Indian would ever harm him or his son and that is what I very firmly believe myself.

"I firmly believe that my husband and son are alive and are being protected, and that they will get away some day, but when I know not...Yes I have had information from various friends in different parts of the globe, who claimed to have received 'telepathic messages' from Col. Fawcett, asking that the messages should be transmitted to me, as he was not able or permitted to communicate with me directly.

"'Around Christmas time I had no less than six messages giving 1931 as the year when we would have important news of them. And yesterday that American lady told me she had received a message at dawn on May 7th from my husband to be given to me and it was to the effect that with certain training I could receive the messages myself from him now.'

"After that Mrs. Fawcett got her own telepathic contact with her husband and she said she was confident that the Colonel and her son would soon reappear with news of tremendous scientific valud to the world.

"I believe that his son Jack was closer to the Subterranean People and that is probably why they disappeared in Matto Grosso. Here's the reason. Fawcett was not just exploring. He had something given by Sir Rider Haggard, author, which was an amulet carved of black basalt, with a plaque on its chest inscribed with mysterious characters. It was believed that it came from a lost prehistoric city, and that is what the Colonel was searching for. This stone idol had a peculiar property. Something like a strong electric current would flow from it up one's arm, so strong and noticeable that some people had to drop it hastily. No one could explain it until a medium who was able to sense the history of the object just by holding it, claimed that the amulet was a portrait of a high priest in Atlantis. It was passed on to appointed ones until it would come into the possession of a reincarnation of the person it portrays. I often wonder if Jack was the owner of the amulet and is the high priest mentioned when Jack was born." (Just before Jack's birth, prior to May 19, 1903, while Fawcett was waiting for his wife, Nina, to give birth, in Colombo, Ceylon, he was approached by a deputation of soothsayers and Buddhists who told him that he was to have a son who was a reincarnation of a very advanced spirit. He would be born on Buddha's anniversary, celebrated in Ceylon on the 19th of May.)

SPACEMEN OR SUBTERRANEAN MEN?

Since the Atlanteans were a race of giants, it is probable that the pilots of flying saucers, some of whom are dwarfs and some our own stature, and evidently of surface origin, are employed by them to make trips into our atmosphere and are instructed to pretend to be "spacemen" for security reasons. True "spacemen" could not look and talk so much like us. It would be the rarest possibility and contrary to all the laws of chance for two different planets, composed of different chemical elements and with different gravitation, climatic, atmospheric and other conditions, could develop two forms of life so identical as these "spacemen" and ourselves. These "spacemen" are certainly far different from what H.G.Wells imagined Martians to be!

What is the explanation for this remarkable similarity? These "spacemen" resemble us because they are not "spacemen" at all. They are of terrestrial origin. If they were once Germans who gained access, after they once gained access to the Subterranean World, they would continue to speak German, as some saucermen spoke. This would be strange if they were "spacemen", because it would be difficult to explain why people of other planets, who speak another language, should perfect their capacity to speak German when they came to visit an English-speaking people. If their intelligence was so high, they should be able to speak all languages if they spoke one. And how could they have learned German millions of miles away, no matter how wonderful were their recording instruments making them more or less omniscient. Besides, even if they learned German, they could not speak it with an accent that only a native-born German could have.

In the case of some saucers that crashed, small men were found among the wreckage, who were claimed to be "small men from Mars". But this is a pure supposition, without any proof. It is much more probable that the subterranean Atlanteans employed subterranean dwarfs as pilots of their flying saucers. Writing in "the little brown men in the flying saucers", Fitch says:

37

"Though smaller than we are, they are much stronger. Their
grip is like a vice. One of them could quickly overpower a strong
man. Their bodies are perfect in build. Both men and women dress
very neatly. Though not beautiful, they are nice looking. Not one
of them looks to be over 30 years old. They say they do not expect
to die. (Since the Eskimos claim that their ancestors came from
within the North Polar opening, the land beyond the Pole, these
small brown men were obviously of the same race as the ancestors
of the Eskimos.)

"It would take a book to record the conversations that have
taken place with the saucermen and women. Their speech is quick,
sharp and right to the point. They seem to be very, very intelligent.
They talk freely and answer all questions, but they lie about things
they do not want us to know (such as claiming they come from other
planets, when they really come from inside the earth).

"Here are a few brief statements or claims made by the little
men and women who live inside this earth. They boast about their
superior mentality and knowledge, and that they excell us in creative
ability. They say they are far ahead of is from the standpoint of
new inventions (of which flying saucers are only one, and perhaps not
by any means the greatest). For instance, they claim that their
flying saucers are powered with 'free energy' (meaning the electromagnetic energy of space, which is free and not like the fuel used
to supply our aircraft). They claim that they obtain this 'free
energy' by exploding certain atoms by action of the electromagnetic
energy of space while in flight.

"They say they are thousands of years ahead of us in all of the
arts, such as paintings, sculpture and archetectural designing.
Also that they are ahead of us in their domestic and business
management, in their agricultural techniques, and that their beautiful landscapes, parks, flower gardens, orchards and farms vastly
surpass our own.

"They claim that they are far ahead of us in their knowledge of
nutrition and in their diet. They claim to live in luxury, yet
have no class distinction, and that there is no poverty or crime
among them, nor need of police. (In this and in all other respects
they closely resemble the subterranean race of advanced vegetarians
described by Bulwer Lytton in his book, "The Coming Race", who
possess a Utopian civilization, far superior to our own.) They say
that their saucermen know every language on earth.

"They teach the same wicked doctrines taught by communism
(advocating common ownership and the abolition of private property,
competition and class distinction, all working together for their
common welfare. Since their doctrines are so much like that of the
communists, this may explain why, while the U.S.Government refused
to admit their existence or have anything to do with them, Russian
scientists were eager to make friends with them, and the USSR
Academy of Science and Space Research admitted the reality of the
flying saucers and claimed they came from Venus, and that some of
them crashed on earth and their pilots were killed. Since the
Russians were more willing to co-operate with them than other nations,
they probably used the Russians to launch a peace offensive for
world disarmament, summit meetings, the banning of nuclear tests and

38

the destruction of nuclear weapons. It is due to their efforts that a nuclear world war that would otherwise have occurred was prevented and that nuclear tests by the major nations were stopped.)

"They say we should get rid of nuclear bombs and armaments. They say we should and will have one world government. They say that all their efforts are for peace. They say that our peace is due to their efforts in our behalf, and that they saved us from being plunged into a suicidal nuclear world war, and that we should look to them for future guidance.

"They say that they are from other planets, but we doubt it. (This is a bluff purposely told to conceal the true where-abouts of their place of origin lest militaristic governments start a race in their direction just as they are now racing in the opposite direction - into space. Yet, rather than attempting to reach the barren moon, if they had any sense, they would try to reach the New World inside the hollow interior of the earth, with a larger land area than our own world. For while 75% of the earth's surface is covered with water, and the present land area is only 55 million square miles out of a total area of the earth's surface of 197 million square miles, Fitch claims that there are no oceans in the interior comparable with those on the exterior of the earth; and if this is so, then there must be three times as much land in the inside of the earth than on the outside, capable of supporting three times its population or rather much more, because while the outer surface, with its cold winters, deserts and droughts, as well as ice-covered polar areas, has only a limited surface and a limited season suitable for agriculture, the interior surface of the earth's crust, which has a climate of perpetual summer, adequate rainfall and no deserts or frozen areas, is capable of much greater agricultural production per square mile of land surface. And in the struggle of the major nations to acquire this El Dorado and claim it as their territory, a war would develop, not only among them but between the subterranean people and the surface invaders, which would be more terrible than any nuclear war could possibly be. It is to prevent such a catastrophe that flying saucer pilots were ordered by their superiors to pretend that they came from outer space and not from their true place of origin, the earth's interior.)

A subterrean tunnel explorer whom the writer met in Santa Catarina told him about a rare book he once came across, written in old German by one of the early German settlers who came to Brazil with the Portuguese, which recorded the traditions that the Indians here acquired from the Atlanteans who once colonized Brazil. This book stated that the earth is hollow and that its hollow interior is inhabited by descendants of the Atlanteans, who compose a disease-free, long-lived race of fruit-eaters, who enjoy a longevity measured in the thousands of years. They are very muscular. In the colonized Brazil. This book stated that the earth is hollow and that its hollow interior is inhabited by descendants of the Atlanteans, who compose a disease-free, long-lived race of fruit-eaters, who enjoy a longevity measured in the thousands of years. They are very muscular. In the center of the hollow interior of the earth, the author said, was a sun, which gave it light and supported plant growth. He also spoke of tunnels that connect the outer surface and the Subterranean World in the hollow interior of the earth, and stated that the greatest number of openings of these tunnels exist in the states of Santa Catarina and Parana, Brazil.

That this is the case the writer has verified after a two year study of the tunnels and alleged subterranean cities of Santa Catarina and Parana. After an unsuccessful trip to Matto Grosso in search of the Roncador opening, on his return to Santa Catarina, where he lives, he was surprised to learn that there are more genuine tunnel openings here, leading to subterranean cities, than in Matto Grosso. The reason for this is because the suboceanic tunnels that went under the Atlantic and connected Atlantis with the coast of South America struct land in Santa Catarina and Parana, after which they connected underneath Brazil to Matto Grosso and then on to Atlantis's Inca colony in Peru. The tunnel route then ran down the Andes to Chile.

Let us quote further what Fitch says about the saucermen, who, he claims, have a subterranean origin:

"They say they know all the secrets of every government. They say they are of higher intelligence and authority. In other words, they boast that they have authority over us, since they are our superiors. They claim to be experts in mental telepathy. They claim that they come from an antediluvian race (Atlantean). They say that they can become invisible. They say that they know nothing at all about Jesus, and say our Bible is mistranslated, misinterpreted and misconstrued. They say they can save man, not from sin, but from himself. They claim they are a race which has not fallen as we have."

IS THE SUBTERRANEAN WORLD THE TRUE SHANGRI-LA?

The following article, entitled "Does Shangri-la Exist?", was written by Professor Henrique J. de Souza, president of the Brazilian Theosophical Society, archeologist and esotericist, in his magazine, "Dharana":

"Among all races of mankind, back to the dawn of time, there existed a tradition concerning the existence of a Sacred Land or Terrestrial Paradise, where the highest ideals of humanity are realized. This ideal is found in the most ancient writings and traditions of the peoples of Europe, Asia Minor, China, India, Egypt and the Americas. This Sacred Land, it is said, is made known only to persons who are worthy, who are pure and innocent, for which reason it constitutes a major theme of the dreams of childhood.

"The road that leads to this blessed land, this invisible world, this esoteric and occult domain, constitutes the master key to all the mystery teachings and systems of initiation of the past, present and future. This magic key is the "Open Sesame" that unlocks the door to a new marvelous world. The old Rosicrucians designated it by the French word VITRION, which is the seven first letters of the words in the sentence: VISITA INTERIORA RECTIFICANDO INVENTIES OMNIA LAPIDEM, to indicate that "in the interior of the earth is hidden the true MYSTERY". The path that leads to this occult world is the Way of Initiation.

"In Ancient Greece, in the Mysteries of Delphos and Eleusis, this heavenly land was referred to as Mount Olympus and the Elysian

Fields. Also in the earliest Vedic times, it was called by various names, such as Tatnasanu (the peak of the precious stone,)Hemadri (the mountain of gold) and Mount Meru,(the home of the gods,)the Olympus of the Hindus. Symbolically, the peak of the sacred mountain is in the sky, its middle part on earth and its base in the Underworld.

"The Scandinavian Eddas mention this celestrial city (Shamballah) which was in the subterranean Land of Asar of the peoples of Mesopotania. It was the Land of Amenti of the sacred Book of the Dead of the ancient Egyptians. It was the city of the Seven Petals of Vishnu, or the City of the Seven Kings of Edom or Eden of Judaic tradition, or in other words, the Terrestrial Paradise. In all Asia Minor, not only in the past, but also today, there exists a belief in a City of Mystery full of marvels, known as SHAMBALLAH (Shamb-Allah), Temple of the Gods). It is also the Erdami of the Tibetans and Mongols.

"The Persians call it Alberdi or Aryana, land of their ancestors. The Hebrews called it Canaan and the Mexicans Tula or Tulan, while the Aztecs called it Maya-Pan. The Spanish Conquerors, who came to America, believed in the existence of such a city and organized many expeditions to find it, calling it El Dorado or City of Gold. They probably learned about it from the aborigines, who called it by the name of Manoa or City whose King Wears Clothing of Gold.

"By the Celts, the holy land was known as "Land of the Mysteries" - Duat or Dananda. A Chinese tradition speaks of Land of Chavin or the City of a Dozen Serpents. It is the Subterranean World, which lies at the roots of heaven. It is the Land of Calcis or Kalki, the famous Colchida for which the Argonauts sought when they set out in search of the Golden Fleece.

"In the Middle Ages, it was referred to as the Isle of Avalon, where the Knights of the Round Table, under the leadership of King Arthur and under the guidance of the magician Merlin, went in search of the Holy Grail, symbol of obedience, justice and immortality. When King Arthur was seriously wounded in battle, he requested his companion Belvedere to depart on a boat to the confines of the earth; with the following words: 'Farewell, friend and companion Belvedere, and go to the land where it never rains, where there is no sickness and where nobody dies.' This is the Land of Immortality or Agharta, the Subterranean World. This land is the Walhalla of the Germans, the Mount Salvat of the Knights of the Holy Grail, the Utopia of Thomas More, the City of the Sun of Campanella, the Shangri-la of Tibet and the Agharta of the Buddhist World."

ORIENTAL TRADITIONS CONCERNING AGHRTA, THE SUBTERRANEAN WORLD

The late Russian explorer Roerich, who spent much of his life in the Himalayas and Tibet, claimed that under the Tibetan capital of Llasa lies a tunnel that connects it with the subterranean world capital of Shamballah, where is the palace of the King of the World, who communicates his orders in this way to the Dalai Lama, his viceroy above. The entrance to this tunnel is well guarded by lamas, who have sworn to keep its actual whereabouts an inviolable secret never communicated to outsiders, by the order of the Dalai Lama himself, who is the terrestrial representative of the ruler of the subterranean empire and paradise, which it is the goal of all lamas to reach.

41

Roerich claimed that somewhere in the Orient existed a shaft reaching far into the earth, by which the Subterranean World of Agharta and its capital city of Shamballah, the heavenly city of the Buddhist world, may be reached. ("Hail Agharta, thou Champion of Shamballah", is a favorite Buddhist expression.) It is probable that Roerich's ceaseless travels in the Himalayan regions, whose purpose he never revealed, were in order to find an entrance to the Subterranean World, for while he and his wife could have lived in comfort, he preferred to endure the rigors of the intensely cold climate of the high Himalayas and Tibet in order to pursue this quest until his very end. Another Slavic explorer who spent many years in this rugged and foreboding terrain, and who was likewise fascinated by Oriental beliefs concerning Agharta and Shamballah, was the Polish scientist, Fernando Ossendowski, author of "Beasts, Men and Gods", in which he presents the fullest account yet given by any Western writer on this subject. From his book we gather the following.

Tribes of Inner Mongolia believe that the Subterranean World of Agharta was the creation of an antediluvian civilization, which exists in the interior of the earth and is reached by tunnels that connect it with the surface through openings that exist in various parts of the world. Tibetan lamas believe that underneath the American continents live a vast population of survivors of the Atlantean catastrophe, who inhabit subterranean cities, which are connected with each other by tunnels, and also that suboceanic tunnels connect the various continents. They also state that these underground cities are illuminated by a green-yellow luminescence which aids underground plant life there and length of human life. Through these tunnels pass subterranean vehicles that travel at incredible speed.

Recently the Brazilian press and radio announced that a party of geologists and other scientists entered one of the many tunnels that open on the tops of mountains here (evidently constructed by an antediluvian race of Atlanteans before the Flood, who did not wish floodwaters to enter), and after descending some distance, came to a subterranean city. Then a sudden fright seized the party, and they fled before they entered the city. They refused to return or to reveal what made them get frightened. Perhaps the city was inhabited and perhaps its inhabitants did not want to be molested and projected certain types of radiations on them.

It is claimed that Atlantis was connected with its Egyptian colony by means of a tunnel whose entrance was in a chamber below the Pyramid of Gizeh. The Egyptian Book of the Dead said: "I am the offspring of yesterday; the tunnels of the earth have given me birth and I am revealed at the appointed time." This refers to Egypt having been a child of Atlantis, and connected with the Motherland by suboceanic and subterranean tunnels. The Book of the Dead also speaks of the "tunnels of Ra". Osiris, the ruler of the Underworld, was a subterranean god. He was probably an Atlantean king who had gone underground, to escape the Flood.

A pilot of a transport from Britist Guiana to Dakar, Africa, one day saw that his ship was following a great Panzar highway, with cities or villages every fifty miles or so, with the sudden realization that they were under water and visible, due to the sea being as smooth as glass, some 500 miles off Dakar.

42

In the chapter of his book referred to above, entitled "The Sub-terranean Empire", Ossendowski writes of the Mystery of Mysteries, pertaining to the Subterranean World of Agharta and its capital city of Shamballah, where dwells the King of the World in his palace, who, when he uttered his prophecy concerning the future of the peoples of earth, caused camels of his caravan to stop and open their ears, horses to become immobile and attentive, cattle to bow down to the ground, birds to stop flying and dogs to bark. "The air vibrated sweetly and carried from afar the music of a song that penetrated to the hearts of men, beasts and birds. "The wind stopped blowing and the sun stood still in its course. Ossendowski writes:

"The oldest inhabitants of the coast of Amyl related to me an old legend according to which a Mongolian tribe, seeking refuge from Gengis Kan, hid in a subterranean cavern. Later a native who lived in the neighborhood of Nogan Kul lake showed me the door that serves as the entrance to the kingdom of Agharta. Once a hunter entered this door and visited the underground empire, and on his return began to relate what he had seen. The lamas cut off his tongue to prevent him from speaking about the Mystery of Mysteries. When he was old, he returned to the entrance of the cavern and disappeared into the subterranean world.

"I obtained from detailed information from the lips of Jelyl Dyamsrap de Narabanchi Kure. He related the history of the arrival of the mighty King of the World and his leaving the Subterranean World, his appearance, miracles and prophecies; and only then I began to understand this legend, this hypnosis, this collective vision, however we interprete it, which envelopes more than one mystery, and is a real and governing force capable of influencing the course of the political life of Asia. As soon as I realized this I commenced my investigations in earnest.

"The lama Gelong, favorite of Prince Chultun Beyli, and the Prince himself, gave me the following description of the Subterranean World:

"More than six thousand years ago, a holy man, with his entire tribe, disappeared into the interior of the earth and were never again seen on the surface. Many men, however, have since visited this mysterious realm: Sakya Muni, Nadur, Gheghen, Paspe, Beber and others. Nobody knows where it is situated. Some say in Afganistan, others in India. All its members are protected against evil and crime does not exist within its frontiers Science has developed in tranquility, and no one lives threatened by destruction. The subterranean people have reached the apex of wisdom. It is a great empire consisting of millions of inhabitants ruled by the King of the World, who com-mands all the forces of Nature, can read the human soul and the great book of destiny. Invisibly he reigns over eight hundred million sub-jects who are willing to obey his orders.

"Prince Chultun Beyli added: 'This kingdom is Agharta and extends through all the subterranean cavities in the entire earth. I have heard a lama sage tell Bogdo Jan that all the subterranean caverns of America are inhabited by an ancient race that has disappeared from the earth's surface. These people and these subterranean cavities are governed by chiefs who are under the supreme authority of the King of the World. There is nothing surprising in this. In the two

43

great oceans of the east and west there once existed two great continents. The waters submerged them and their inhabitants found refuge in the Subterranean World. The profound caverns are illuminated by a special form of light that permits the growth of cereals and vegetables, which give to the subterranean people a long life free from disease. There exist many races and tribes.'

"The Lama Turgut, who accompanied me on my trip from Urga to Pekin, gave me further information. The capital of Agharta is surrounded by villas in which live the great priests and wise men. It reminds one of Llasa, where is the palace of the Dalai Lama, the Potala, which is on top of a mountain covered with temples and monasteries. The throne of the King of the World is among millions of incarnated gods. The palace itself is surrounded by the residences of the Goros (high priests of the King of the World), who dominate all the visible and invisible forces of the earth, and have in their hands the life and death of all men. If our crazy humanity starts a war against them, they can cause us to disappear from the earth, and to transform its surface into a desert. They can dry seas, alter the configuration of continents and change them into oceans, and level mountains. At their command, trees and vegetation take on new growth, old and weak men are rejuvenated and the dead return to life. In strange vehicles, which we do not know, they travel with tremendous velocity through tunnels that honeycomb the interior of the planet.

"Certain Brahmans of India and some Dalai Lamas of Tibet ascended to the peaks of the cordilleras, never before trodden by human foot, and they saw inscriptions carved on the rocks, footsteps in the snow and tracks made by the wheels of carriages. Sakya Muni found on top of a mountain stone tablets whose letters showed a very advanced age, and then he entered the realm of Agharta. There, in marvelous crystal palaces, live the invisible rulers of the empire: the King of the World, Brahytma and his auxilaries; Mahytma, who can read the future, and Mahynga.

"These holy sages study the world and its forces. At times the most wise unite and send delegates to places where human vision never penetrated. This was described by Sashi Lama, who lived for eight hundred and fifty years."

"Has anyone seen the King of the World?", Ossendowski asked a lama.

"Yes", answered the lama. "During the solemn feasts of primitive Buddhism, in Siam and India, the King of the World appeared five times. He rode in a magnificent carriage drawn by white elephants, enveloped with fine draperies inscribed with gold. The king wore a white robe and on his head a red crown. He blessed the people, whereupon the blind recovered their vision, the deaf heard, the lame began to walk and the dead turned in their tombs. Also, 150 years ago, he appeared in Erdeni Dzu, and visited the old monasteries of Sakki and Narabanchi Kure.

"How many persons have entered Agharta?", I asked the lama.

"'Many', he replied, 'but all guard the secret of what they saw. When the Oletos destroyed Lhasa, one of their regiments, traversing the mountains of the southeast, came to the limits of Agharta. They learned certain mysterious sciences and brought them up to the earth's surface. That is why the Oletos and Kulmucos are such good magicians and fortune-tellers. Certain dark tribes of the East established residence in Agharta for several centuries. They were later expulsed and returned to the earth's surface, possessing the knowledge of fortune-telling by cards, herbs and the lines of the hand. From these tribes came the gypsies. In the north of Asia is a tribe, which is becoming extinct, that resided in marvelous Agharta.'

"Many times the priests of Urga and Lhasa sent embassadors to the court of the King of the World. A certain Tibetan warrior, after a battle with the Oletos, came to a cavern on which was the famous inscription: 'This door leads to Agharta." From the cavern came out a fine-looking man who showed a golden tablet on which was writing in an unknown language and said:

"'The King of the World will appear before men when will come the hour when the good will start their battle against the evil, but that hour has not yet come. The worse of humanity have yet to be born.'

"The baron Ungern sent as an ambassador to the realm of Agharta the young prince Punzig, but he came back with a letter from the Dalai Lama of Llasa. The baron sent him a second time but he never returned."

PROPHECY OF THE COMING NUCLEAR ARMEGEDDON
BY THE KING OF THE WORLD

Delivered in 1890 to the Lamas of a Monstery in the Far East, Predicting the Annihilation of all Inhabitants of the Earth's Surface and that its only Survivors will be Those who Found Refuge from Radioactivity in the Subterranean World

The following prophecy by the King of the World was related to Ossendowski by the Hutukta of Narabanchi, whose monstery he visited in 1921, who related the visit of the King of the World to the lamas there a little over 30 years previously, when he delivered the following prophecy of the Coming Nuclear Armegeddon and the extermination of surface humanity, leaving the earth inhabited only by its subterranean inhabitants.

When will these direful events occur? Mayita, prophetess of Puerto Rico, and Lavagnini, astrologer of Mexico City, both point to 1965 as the fateful year when the Nuclear Armegeddon of World War III will both commence and be over with, followed by the Four Horsemen of the Apocalypse, involving a Flood of Radioactive Fire followed by a Flood of Water, which will purge and purify the earth's surface, leaving it devoid of life, until eventually the subterranean people will once more come up to the surface and repopulate it. The prophecy of the King of the World, describing these events, was as follows:

"Each day men will increasingly forget their souls and occupy themselves with their bodies. The greatest corruption will reign on earth. Men will resemble ferocious beasts, thirsty for the blood of their fellows. The crowns of kings, great and small, will fall. There will be a terrible war among all the peoples of earth. The

45

oceans will be red with blood. The surface of the earth and the
bottom of the sea will be covered with corpses. Empires will disintegrate; entire nations will disappear. Hunger, disease and crimes
formerly unknown will stalk the land. He who cuts off the arm of the
other will perish too. The ignored and the persecuted will survive
and will attract the attention of the entire world. There will be
terrible fogs and storms. Mountains will fall. The earth will
tremble. Millions will change the chains of slavery and humilitation
for those of hunger, disease and death. The highways will be filled
with multitudes aimlessly running here and there in search of safety.
The largest and most beautiful cities will disappear in flames.

"Father will battle against son, brother against brother and
mother against daughter. Vice, crime and the destruction of body and
soul will proceed without limit. Families will break up and all
fidelity and love will disappear. From ten thousand men, only one
will survive - insane, naked, hungry and without strength, who will
not know how to construct a house or prepare his food. He will roam
like a ravenous wolf, devouring cadavers and biting in his own flesh
in desperation, cursing God.

"The earth will be depopulated. Only night and death will reign.
Then will arise a new people hitherto unknown. With a strong arm
they will uproot the weeds of insanity and vice and will lead those
who remain in the battle of good against evil. They will found a new
life on earth, purified by the health of nations...The people of
Agharta will leave their subterranean caverns and once more will
appear upon the surface of the earth."

WORLDS BEYOND THE POLES AND THE MYSTERY OF ADMIRAL BYRD'S FLIGHT

The December 1959 issue of "FLYING SAUCERS" magazine, published
by Ray Palmer was mysteriously removed from circulation. When the
truck arrived to deliver the magazines from the printer to the publisher, no magazines were found in it. A phone call to the printer
resulted in his not finding any way-bill proving shipment to have
taken place. The magazines having been paid for, the publisher asked
that the printer return the plates to the press and run off the
copies due. But strangely, the plates were not available, and were
so badly damaged that no re-runs could be made. But where were the
thousands of magazines that were printed and which mysteriously
disappeared? Why was there no way-bill? If it was lost and the
magazines were sent to a wrong address, they would turn up somewhere.
But they did not.

Thus 5000 subscribers did not get the magazine. One distributor,
who received 750 copies, was reported missing, and the 750 magazines
disappeared with him, which were sent to him with the request they
be returned if not delivered. They did not come back. Since the
magazine disappeared, several months later it was republished and
sent to subscribers.

Now, what did this magazine contain that caused it to be suppressed by some secret agency? It contained a report of Admiral
Byrd's secret flight over the North Pole in 1947, based on information
derived from Giannini's book "WORLDS BEYOND THE POLES", published
in 1959 by Vantage Press, New York. For some strange reason the

publisher, after printing the book, made no effort to advertise it, and it remained almost unknown until Ray Palmer gave it publicity in his December 1959 issue of "FLYING SAUCERS", which so strangely disappeared. It seemed that some black hand stopped the publisher from doing anything about the book after he printed it.

This book is the only published record of an airplane flight made by Rear Admiral Richard E. Byrd beyond the North Pole in February, 1947. Now this word "beyond" is significant. It does not mean "across" the North Pole to the other side, but means into an unknown land, not recorded on any map, that is reached by traveling north, and, after passing the North Pole, still going north, as Admiral Byrd is supposed to have done for 1700 miles, Describing this flight, Palmer, in his suppressed Dec. 1959 issue of "FLYING SAUCERS", described as follows what he called "the best-kept secret in history":

"In February of that year (1947), Admiral E. Byrd, the one man who has done the most to make the North Pole a known area, made the following statement: 'I'd like to see that land beyond the Pole. That area beyond the Pole is the center of the great unknown."

"Millions of people read his statement in their daily newspapers. And millions thrilled to the Admiral's subsequent flight to the Pole and to a point 1700 miles beyond it. Millions heard the radio broadcast description of that flight, which was also published in the newspapers. Briefly, for the benefit of our readers, we will recount that flight as it progressed. When the plane took off from its Arctic base, it proceeded straight north to the Pole. From that point, it flew on a total of 1700 miles beyond the Pole, and then retraced its course to its Arctic base. As progress was made beyond the Pole point, iceless land and lakes, mountains covered with trees and even a monstrous animal moving through the underbrush, were observed and reported via radio by the plane's occupants. For almost all of the 1700 miles, the plane flew over land, mountains, trees, lakes, rivers.

"What land was it? Look at your map. Calculate the distance to the Pole from all the known lands we have previously mentioned (Siberia, Spitzbergen, Alaska, Canada, Finland, Norway, Greenland and Iceland). A good portion of them are well within the 1700 mile range. But none of them are within 200 miles of the Pole. Byrd flew over no known land. He himself called it 'the great unknown'. And great it is, indeed! For after 1700 miles over land, he was forced by gasoline supply limit to return, and he had not yet reached the end of it! He should have been well inside one of the known areas mentioned. He should have been back to 'civilization'. But he was not. He should have seen nothing but ice-covered ocean, or at the very most, partially open ocean. Instead he was over mountains covered with forests.

"Forests!

"Incredible! The northernmost limit of the timber-line is located well down into Alaska, Canada and Siberia. North of that line no tree grows! All around the North Pole, the tree does not grow within 1700 miles of the Pole!

"What have we here? We have the well-authenticated flight of Admiral Richard E. Byrd to a land beyond the Pole that he so much wanted to see, because it was the center of the unknown, the center of mystery. Apparently, he had his wish gratified to the fullest, yet today, in 1959, nowhere is that mysterious land mentioned. Why? Was that 1947 flight fiction? Did all the newspapers lie? Did the radio from Byrd's plane lie?

"No, Admiral Byrd did fly beyond the Pole.

"Beyond?"

"What did the Admiral mean when he used that word? How is it possible to go 'beyond' the Pole? Let us consider for a moment: Let us imagine that we are transported by some miraculous means, to the exact point of the North Magnetic Pole. We arrive there instantaneously, not knowing from which direction we came. And all we know is that we are to proceed from the Pole to Spitzbergen. But where is Spitzbergen? Which way do we go? South, of course! But which south? All directions from the North Pole are south!

"This is actually a simple navigational problem. All expeditions to the Pole, whether flown, or by submarine, or on foot, have been faced with this problem. Either they must retrace their steps, or discover which southerly direction is the correct one to their destination, whatever it has been determined to be. The problem is solved by making a turn, in any direction, and proceeding approximately 20 miles. Then we stop, shoot the stars, correlate with out compass reading (which no longer points straight down, but toward the North Magnetic Pole), and plot our course on the map. Then it is a simple matter to proceed to Spitzenbergen by going south.

"Admiral Byrd did not follow this traditional navigational procedure: when he reached the Pole, he continued on for 1700 miles. To all intents and purposes, he continued on a northerly course, after crossing the Pole. And weirdly, it stands on the record that he succeeded, for he did see that 'land beyond the Pole' which to this day, if we are to scan the records of newspapers, book, radio, television and word of mouth, has never been revisited!

"That land, on today's maps, cannot exist. But since it does, we can only conclude that today's maps are incorrect, incomplete, and do not present a true picture of the Northern Hemisphere.

"Having thus located a great land mass in the North, not on any map today, a land which is the center of the great unknown, which can only be construed to imply that the 1700 mile extent traversed by Byrd is only a portion of it..."

Obviously, certain secret agencies considered the above information sufficient reason to suppress the December 1959 issue of "FLYING SAUCERS" in an effort to withhold the information it contained from the public. Who are these agencies and why did they wish to withhold this information, which, evidently, had already appeared in the press and radio some years previously? Was it that the U.S. Government had its eye on this unknown territory ever since Byrd first discovered it, and wished the matter hushed, so that it could claim it before the Russians; and for this reason tried to suppress the magazine from circulation.

Now in this connection it is interesting to note that a certain flying saucer writers, as Jarrold and Bender, who wrote about the "Antarctic Mystery", namely the strange concentration of flying saucers which were seen to ascend and descend from a certain point in the Antarctic, were visited by "three men in black", who immediately muzzled them and caused them to suspend further mention of this matter. Recently Dr. George Marlo, director of U.F.O. World Research, reported that Buck Nelson, who has been publicizing his flying saucer trip, was beaten up by these same "three men in black", who had threatened to beat Jarrad and Bender if they kept talking. A few days ago, Dr. Marlo wrote he was visited by five FBI lately in reference to his flying saucer trips through the North Polar opening into the earth's interior, which he has claimed to make. This is a surprising admission that the FBI take the matter seriously, for if they regarded Dr. Marlo as another crackpot talking through his hat, they would not bother to visit him for the purpose of muzzling him. Marlo writes he is now being hounded day and night, due to his statements about visiting the "land beyond the Pole."

Now the mystery deepens when we read in the February 1960 issue of "FLYING SAUCERS" the following:

"The one big flaw in our now 'most-talked-of' issue ever, the December 1959 'mystery Polar lands' issue, is the non-existent North Pole flight of Admiral Byrd in 1947. We don't know how many of our readers caught up on this, and proved that Admiral Byrd did NOT make a flight beyond the North Pole in February 1947. The fact is, of course, and we admit it freely, that the February 1947 flight was a SOUTH POLE flight, just as was the 1957 flight. The only flight Admiral Byrd made over the North Pole was in 1926, and in it, he merely flew to the Pole, CIRCLED it twice, then returned to Base,

"Almost unanimously, our readers who detected this flaw asked us HOW it could happen that we could make such a serious error, after our years of research into this thing, and particularly since we said we wanted to be sure of our facts before we presented our 'Earth is not round' theory. They pointed out that we had seriously impaired the validity of our theory if the North Pole is perfectly normal, then our theory about the South Pole might be damaged.

"There are two alternatives - either Byrd made a SECRET flight over the North Pole in 1947, which NEVER hit the newspapers, or a deliberate effort was being made to build up an edifice that could be toppled IF AND WHEN THE TRUTH CAME OUT ABOUT THE SOUTH POLE!

"As it actually turned out, Byrd did NOT make a North Pole flight 1700 miles beyond the Pole - but he DID make a South Pole flight 1700 miles beyond the SOUTH Pole! We had hoped that more of our readers would notice that we had, in our research, not discovered the 1947 South Polar flight, which would be strange indeed, because it sticks out like a sore thumb all over the newspaper, magazine and book world! Reams have been written of that flight. Our alibi, if we wished to use one, could have been that it was simply a typographical error, and we meant South Pole all the time, and not North. But then somebody would have popped up and said - but this is ridiculous, because of all your specific mention of the areas around the North Pole.

"No, we aren't presenting any alibi - what we are presenting is possibly the missing fact we were searching for all along; that to this day, no attempt has been made to fly beyond the North Pole, but that every trip to the Pole had followed the standard navigational procedure which we pointed out must invariably turn you away from any land 'beyond' and bring you back on a southerly course which will bring you inevitably to a known land. Byrd, in 1926, flew to the North Pole, circled it twice (it took about five minutes to fly these two circles) and then headed back to his starting point!

"When we read of Admiral Byrd's amazing 1947 NORTH Pole flight 1700 miles BEYOND the Pole, and compared its startling similarity to the actual 1947 SOUTH Pole flight, which went the same distance beyond the South Pole, we found ourselves with an obvious paradox, yet not an impossible one. There were two weeks' possible difference in time of both flights, and Byrd COULD have made them both. The question is, DID HE? We had absolutely no way of knowing. We reasoned thusly: If by chance Byrd actually kept secret, but in some obscure publication it 'leaked' out, but was covered up so successfully that we had been unable to discover the 'leak', we might find one of our readers sending us the material in question, possibly dug from yellowing newspapers in his attic. No suchconfirmation was forthcoming, but much information correcting our error was.

"Where did we get our information on Byrd's non-existent North Pole flight and 1700 mile penetration beyond it in 1947? Yes, it WAS published, and in a very strange book. We feel that now we can reveal the book, and its information, and ask our readers but one question - isn't this the PERFECT book to make a laughing stock out of anyone who happens to come up with out 'mystery land at the Poles' theory?

"We doubt if this book enjoyed a large sale. We doubt, in fact, if it has achieved even a slight sale. Our two copies came to us as 'review copies' from the publisher. We have not seen it publicized anywhere. We have not heard of any of our readers buying it.

"The title of this strange book is 'Worlds Beyond the Poles' ($3.50), its author F. Amadeo Giannini. It was published by Vantage Press, Inc., 120 W. 31st Street, New York 1, N.Y., on July 6, 1959. In it, not only is the 1947 NORTH Pole flight of 1700 miles beyond the Pole in a northerly direction completely described, but it is the Pole in a northerly direction completely described, but it is reiterated over and over again, with complete quotes from newspapers, radio, etc.

"Because of this positivism, your editor could not conceive that either Giannini or Vantage Press could have made so disturbing a 'typographical error' because of the very facts we mentioned before which would render the same claim on our part invalid, namely the direct reference to North Polar adjacent lands. There are two possibilities - that Giannini was deliberately falsifying, or it was true that he had access to information your editor did not, and in fact, could not verify no matter how intensely he searched. There was only one thing to do - to pass this on my own information, so that no one would suspect the existence of the Giannini book, and discover, if I could, if anybody ELSE than Giannini had possession of actual information regarding the contradictory flight. Since nothing has turned up (and it should have, if true, because our readers turned every library in the country upside down in an effort to either confirm our claims, or to disprove them), we can only conclude the first alternative; that Giannini deliberately falsified. The big question is WHY?

"Briefly, for our reader's information, Giannini claims the Earth is just a part of a continuous land area which comprises the entire universe and that the access to such seemingly disassociated worlds as Mars, the Moon, other planets is via the Poles, which are continuous terra firma extending upward the outward into 'space'; so that the only sensible way to go to the moon is but by rocket, as the Russians did, but by motor car (or tractor if the going is rough) into the sky on the spindle-shaped Poles of the earth.

"Yet, throughout the book there exists the whole gamut of strange facts which we ourselves had been aware of for years, all carefully mustered to support a theory doomed by every process of logic to be forever incomprehensible. No one, reading the book, will seriously hold the 'land continuity' theory he expresses as for even a moment. In fact, if he reads the entire book, he will once and for all, faced with legitimate points in the book, refuse to consider them for any other purpose because of the illegitimacy that has 'rubbed off' on them by association with the weird 'continuity' theory Giannini apparently seriously puts forth.

"Perhaps the reader can imagine the emotions of this editor, after twenty years of useful assembly of facts preparatory to lauching a theory of the lack of true concept of the shape of our Earth, when he found many of the impressive items in his arsenal firing resounding salvos of blanks in support of the utterly ridiculous. Now, to use the same items in support of what amounts to an exactly diametric theory; i.e., that the Earth is strangely shaped at the poles, either in a dish-shaped depression of huge dimensions, or a hole all the way through, with the resultant Earth distinctly doughnut-shaped, seems almost folly.

"The fact is, now that it seems sure that Giannini falsified the Byrd North Pole flight, no human being has ever flown directly over the NORTH Pole and continued straight on, as has been done at the South Pole...Many of our readers stated that even commercial flights continually cross the Pole and fly to the opposite side of the Earth. This is just not true, and though the Airline officials themselves, when asked, might say that they do, it is not literally true. They DO make the navigational maneuvers which automatically eliminate a flight beyond the Pole in a straight line, in every case. Ask the pilots of these Polar flights. And when you come to pin it right down, name ONE trans-polar flight on which you can buy a ticket today. Not just a flight from New York to Gander New Foundland, and on out over the Atlantic to Ireland, or any other flight you can find on the travel schedule of any airline in the world - but a flight which actually crosses the North Pole."

Examining the routes of flights across the North Polar area we always find that they go around the Pole or to the side of it and never directly across it. This is strange. Surely a flight advertised as passing directly over the North Pole would attract many passengers who would like to have that experience. Yet, strangely,

no airline offers such a flight. Their air routes always pass on one
side of the Pole. Why? Is it not possible that if they went straight
across the Pole, inside of landing on the opposite side of the Earth,
the plane would go to that land beyond the Pole, 'the center of the
great unknown' as Admiral Byrd called it? In fact, Palmer suggests
that such an expedition, to fly directly north past the North Pole,
after passing over it, be immediately organized, retracing Byrd's
route. He writes:

"The strange book written by Giannini has offered the one possibility by which it can definitely be proved that the Earth is shaped
strangely at the North Pole, as we believe it to be at the South Pole,
not necessarily with a hole all the way through, but like a doughnut
which swelled so much in cooking that the hole is only a deep depression at each end, or like a gigantic auto tire mounted on a solid
hub with recessed hub caps. The fact is, now that it seems sure that
Giannini falsified the Byrd North Pole flight, no human being has ever
flown directly over the North Pole, and continued straight on, as has
been done at the South Pole. Your editor thinks it should be done,
and done immediately. We have the planes to do it...Your editor wants
to know for sure, whether such a flight would wind up in any of the
countries surrounding the North Pole, necessarily exactly opposite
the starting point. Navigation is not to be made by compass, or by
triangulation on existing maps, but solely by gyro compass on an
undeviating straight course from the moment of take-off to the moment
of landing. And not only a gyro in a horizontal plane, but one in a
vertical plane also. There must be a positive forward motion which
cannot be disputed."

Everyone knows that a horizontal gyro compass, such as used now,
causes a plane continually to gain in elevation as the earth surves
away below it as it progresses. Now, according to our theory of a
polar depression, this would mean that when a plane enters into this
depression, the gyro compass should show a much greater gain in
elevation than should otherwise be the case, due to the earth curving
inward at the North Pole. Now, if the plane continues in a northerly
course, this gain in altitude will continue the further it goes; and
if the plane tries to maintain the same altitude, it will curve into
the hollow interior of the earth.

ADMIRAL BYRD'S JOURNEY FOR 2300 MILES BEYOND THE SOUTH POLE.
The press and radio of February 9, 1956 gave the following announcement: "On January 13, members of the United States expedition
accomplished a flight of 2,700 miles from the base at McMurado
Sound, which is 400 miles west of the South Pole, and penetrated a
land extent of 2300 miles beyond the Pole."

On March 13, 1956, Admiral Byrd reported, upon his return from
the South Pole, "The present expedition has opened up a vast new land!

Finally, in 1957, before his death, he described this land as
follows: "That enchanted continent in the sky, land of everlasting
mystery!" Ray Palmer comments on this statement: "Which statement
remains to your editors as the most mysterious of all, and almost
inexplicable. 'Enchanted continent in the sky"...Everlasting mystery
indeed!

"Considering all this, is there any wonder that all the nations of the world have suddenly found the South Polar region (particularly) because of its known land area and the North Pole region so intensely interesting and important, and have launched expeditions on a scale actually tremendous in scope?

"And was it because of Admiral Byrd's weird flight into an unknown Polar land in 1947 that the International Geophysical Year was conceived in that year, and finally brought to fruition ten years later, and is actually still going on? Did his flight make it suddenly imperative to discover the real nature of this planet on which we live, and solve the tremendous mysteries that unexpectedly confronted us?"

In the light of the above, the following quotations from Gianninis book are interesting:

"Since December 12, 1928, U.S.Navy polar expeditions have determined the existence of indeterminable land extent beyond both Pole points.

"Since December 12, 1928, U.S.Navy polar expeditions have determined the existence of indeterminable land extent beyond both Pole points...On January 13, 1956, as this book was being prepared, a U.S.Naval air unit penetrated to the extent of 2,300 miles beyond the assumed South Pole end of the Earth. That flight was always over land and water and ice. For very substantial reasons, the memorable flight received negligible press notice.

"The United States and more than thirty other nations prepared unprecedented polar expeditions for 1957-1958 to penetrate land now proved to extend without limit beyond both Pole points. My original disclosure of then-unknown land beyond the Poles, in 1926-1928, was captioned by the press as 'more daring than anything Jules Verne ever conceived.'

"1947: February. 'I'd like to see that land beyond the Pole. That area beyond the Pole is the center of the great unknown!' - Rear Admiral Richard E. Byrd, U.S.N., before his seven-hour flight over land beyond the North Pole.

"1956: January 13. 'On January 13 members of the United States expedition accomplished a flight of 2,700 miles from the base at McMurdo South, which is 400 miles west of the South Pole, and penetrated a land extent of 2,300 miles beyond the Pole." - Radio announcement, confirmed by the press of February 5.

"March 13. 'The present expedition has opened up a vast new land.' -Admiral Byrd, after returning from land beyond the South Pole.

1957 '...that enchanted continent in the sky, land of everlasting mystery!' - Admiral Byrd.

Giannini states as follows, on page 17 of his book, the error that Palmer quoted in his December 1959 issue of "FLYING SAUCERS":

"Confirmation of such a flight course is had in that of the U.S.Navy task force of February 1947, which penetrated 1,700 miles beyond the North Pole point, and beyond the known Earth. Additional and more recent confirmation was acquired by the flight of a U.S. Navy air unit on January 13, 1956, which penetrated 2,300 miles over land beyond the South Pole.

"There is no physical end to the Earth's northern and southern extent...The Earth cannot be circumnavigated north and south within the meaning of 'circumnavigate'. However, certain 'around the world' flights have contributed to popular misconception that the Earth has been circumnavigated north and south.

"'Over the North Pole', with return to North Temperate Zone areas without turning around can never be accomplished because there is no northern end to the Earth. The same conditions hold true for the South Pole. All progressive movement beyond the respective Pole points leads beyond the assumed 'ends' of an 'isolated globe' Earth.

"This is not 1927. The existence of worlds beyond the Poles has been confirmed by U.S.Naval exploration during the thirty years since then. The confirmation is most substantial, though information has been divulged from every rostrum. They of the rostrums are as little informed of the meaning of polar exploration as members of the press.

"It was disclosed that the world's elder explorer, Rear Admiral Richard Evelyn Byrd, was to command the government's memorable expedition into that endless land beyond the South Pole...Prior to his departure from San Francisco he delivered the momentous radio announcement, 'This is the most important expedition in the history of the world.' The subsequent January 13, 1956, penetration of land beyond the Pole to the extent of 2,300 miles proved that the admiral had not been exaggerating."

DID COOK OR PEARY OR NEITHER DISCOVER THE
NORTH POLE?

Dr. Frederick A. Cook, on April 21, 1908, announced that he had reached the North Pole. His announcement was followed by a few days by one from Rear Admiral Robert E. Peary, who claimed he reached the Pole on April 6, 1909. Both men hurled accusations against the other claiming that they discovered the Pole and the other did not. Cook accused Peary saying that he had appropriated some of his stories cached against his return from the Pole. Cook, in his turn, failed to supply notes he said he had kept of his trip, and thereby cast doubt on his own story.

Although Cook claims to have been the first to reach the Pole, Peary is generally believed to have done so. Cook's claim was discredited because the sun altitude was so low that observations of it as proof of the position were worthless. Peary reached, or rather claimed he reached, the Pole in April, 15 days earlier in the season, and therefore under even more adverse solar conditions. His calculations are therefore more suspect than Cook's. Cook, it was said, had no witnesses other than Eskimos. The same is true of Peary. Peary, however, lacked witnesses through choice, having ordered his white companions to remain behind, while he went on alone with one Eskimo companion to the Pole. Cook was doubted in his claim to have averaged 15 miles a day. Peary claimed to have made over 20. The argument is still not perfectly settled.

There is one factor in Peary's dash to the Pole that casts suspicion on his claim to have reached it. It was the remarkable speed at which he claimed to travel or would have to travel to reach it and return during the time he did. When he neared the 88th parallel, he decided to attempt the final dash to the Pole in five days. He made 25 miles the first day; 20 on the second; 20 on the third; 25 on the fourth; 40 on the fifth. His five-day average was 26 miles. On the return trip he traveled a total of 153 miles in 2 days, including a halt 5 miles from the Pole to take a sounding of the ocean depth. This is an average of 76½ miles per day. His actual traveling time was approximately 19 hours per day. This is a walking speed of 4 miles per hour. Can a man walk that fast under the incredible conditions of the North Pole area, an ice-terrain described by the men of the atomic submarine "Skate" as fantastically jumbled and jagged? And yet, further south, with presumably better going, he was able to average only 20 miles per day.

From these facts we must conclude that neither Cook nor Peary reached the true North Pole, since it does not exist. Peary may have traveled for the distance calculated as correct to reach the North Pole, but what he really did was to travel this same distance into the depression or opening that exists in this part of the Earth; and the further he would travel, the deeper he would go into this opening, without ever reaching the true Pole.

THE MYSTERY OF TROPICAL MAMMOTHS IN THE ARCTIC

One of the most puzzling facts of Arctic exploration is that while the area is oceanic, covered with water, which is variously frozen over or partially open, depending on the time of the year, many explorers remarked however, paradoxically, that the open water exists in greater measure at the nearer reaches of the Pole. In fact, some explorers found it very hot going at times, and were forced to shed their Arctic clothing. There is even one record of an encounter with naked Eskimos. Yet with this confirmed oceanic area, we have the contradiction of Admiral Byrd's flight being almost entirely over land, mountains covered with trees and interspersed with lakes and streams, and with animal life. One of the reports from the Byrd expedition was the sighting of a huge animal with dark fur. Are there such animals in the Arctic? Palmer believes that this animal, seen by the Byrd expedition, is related to the tropical mammoths, remains of which have been found in the Arctic region, which he believes are Inner Earth animals that have come out through the Arctic opening.

Beginning in Siberia, along the Lena River, there lie exposed on the soil, and buried within it, the bones and tusks of literally millions of mammoths and mastodons. The consensus of scientific opinion is that these are prehistoric remains, and that the mammoth existed some 20,000 years ago, and was wiped out in the unknown catastrophe we now call the last Ice Age. In 1799, a fisherman named Schumachoff, living in Tongoose (Siberia), discovered a complete mammoth frozen in a clear block of ice. Hacking it free, he despoiled it of its huge husks, and left the carcass of fresh meat to be devoured by wolves. Later an expedition set out to examine it and today its skeleton may still be seen in the Museum of Natural History in Petrograd.

In the stomach of the mammoth was found undigested food consisting of young shoots of pine and fir and young fir cones. In others are found fern and tropical vegetation. How could an Arctic animal have tropical food in its stomach? One explanation is that the Arctic region once had a tropical climate, and that a shifting of the Earth on its axis suddenly brought on the Ice Age and changed the climate to a frigid one.

This theory has been offered to explain both the tropical vegetation in the stomach of Arctic animals and the fact that many of these huge prehistoric animals were of tropical species, being related to elephants. Great deposits of elephant tusks were found in Siberia as evidence of the then northern habitat of tropical animals. But there is another theory to explain these facts: that these prehistoric tropical animals came from the interior of the Earth, which has a tropical climate, coming out through the North Polar opening; and since animals of the interior are larger than those of the surface, unaccustomed to the cold climate, they died and froze. Speaking of the death of these animals, Palmer does not accept the axis shift and change of climate theory, and believes these animals came from the Earth's interior. He says:

"True the death must have been sudden, but it was not of tropic locale. If not tropic, then the Ice Age onset is not the cause of death. The cause of death, then, is Arctic in nature, and could have occurred any time. Since the Ice Age there have been no mammoths in the known world. Unless they exist in the mysterious land beyond the Pole, where one of them was actually seen alive by members of the Byrd expedition!

"We have taken taken the mammoth as a rather sensational modern evidence of Byrd's mysterious land, but there are many lesser proofs that an unknown originating point exists somewhere in the northern reaches. We will merely list a few, suggesting that the reader, in examining the records of polar explorers for the past two centuries, will find impossible to reconcile with the known areas of food mentioned early in this presentation of facts, those areas surrounding the Polar Area on your present-day maps.

"The musk-ox, contrary to expectations, migrates north in the wintertime. Repeatedly, Arctic explorers have observed bears heading north into an area where there cannot be food for them. Foxes also are found north of the 80th parallel, heading north, obviously well-fed. Without exception, Arctic explorers agree that the further north one goes, the warmer it gets. Invariably a north wind brings warmer weather. Coniferous trees drift ashore from out of the north. Butterflies and bees are found in the far north, but never hundreds of miles further south; not until Canadian and Alaskan climate areas conducive to such insect life are reached.

"Unknown varieties of flowers are found. Birds resembling snipe, but unlike any known species of bird, come out of the north, and return there. Hare are plentiful in an area where no vegetation ever grows, but where vegetation appears as drifting debris from the

56

northern open waters. Eskimo tribes, migrating northward, have left unmistakable traces of their migration in their temporary camps, always advancing northward. Southern Eskimos themselves speak of tribes that live in the far north. The Ross gull, common at Point Barrow, migrates in October toward the north. Only Admiral Byrd's 'mystery land' can amount for these inexplicable facts and migrations.

"The Scandinavian legend of a wonderful land far to the North called 'Ultima Thule' (commonly confused today with Greenland) is significant when studied in detail, because of its remarkable resemblance to the kind of land seen by Byrd, and its remarkable far north location. To assume that Ultima Thule is Greenland is to come face to face with the contradiction of the Greenland Ice Cap, which fills the entire Greenland basin to a depth of 10,000 feet. A green, fertile land in this location places itself so deep in antiquity that it postules an overturn of the Earth and a new North Pole area...Is Admiral Byrd's land of mystery, center of the great unknown, the same as the Ultima Thula of the Scandinavian legends?

"There are mysteries concerning the Antarctic also. Perhaps the greatest is the highly technical one of biology itself; for on the New Zealand and South American land masses are identical fauna and flora which could not have migrated from one to the other, but rather are believed to have come from a common motherland. That motherland is believed to be the Antarctic Continent. But on a more 'popular' level is the case of the sailing vessel Gladys, captained by F.B.Hatfield in 1893. The ship was completely surrounded by icebergs at 43 degrees south and 33 degrees west. At this latitude an iceberg was observed which bore a large quantity of sand and earth, and which revealed a beaten track, a place of refuge formed in a sheltered nook, and the bodies of five dead men who lay on different parts of the berg. Bad weather prevented any attempts at further investigation.

"Bear in mind that it is an unanimous concensus of opinion among scientists that the one thing peculiar to the Antarctic is that there are no human tribes living upon it. But this concensus must be wrong, because investigation showed that no vessel was lost in the Antarctic at that time so that these dead men could not have been shipwrecked sailors. Even today, with Antarctic exploration at its height, the lack of human life on that bleak continent is agreed upon. Could it be that these men who died on that berg came from 'that mysterious land beyond the South Pole' discovered by the Byrd expedition? Had they ventured out of their warm, habitable land and lost their way along the ice shelf, finally to be drifted to their deaths at sea on a portion of it, broken away to become an iceberg while they were on it?

"Let us go back to Admiral Peary: his astounding rate of travel on his return from the Pole. If he were traveling over the inner lip of a 'doughnut' shape, his bearings would indicate a great distance traveled, due to the foreshortened horizon, and the 'expanded' angle used in making his trigonometrical calculations. Actually he would be traveling the same distance each day, and the drop in speed would be entirely compatible with the bearing observations taken with a constantly lengthening horizon.

"Rocket scientists have made such of the discovery of the

Van Allen Belt, which is a belt of radiation surrounding the Earth. The reader is invited to read about it in the <u>Scientific American</u>, and especially note the drawings of its shape, which is precisely a vast 'doughnut', with the spherical Earth pictured at its center, in the 'hole' of the doughnut. What if the Earth is not spherical, but actually doughnut-shaped, exactly as its surrounding Van Allen Belt? Whatever makes the belt thusly shaped, might it not also be responsible for the shaping of the Earth similarly?

"The evidence is extremely strong, and amazingly prolific in scope and extent, that the Earth actually is shaped in this fashion. And if it is hollow, then we no longer need look for the saucers from outer space - but rather from the 'inner space'! And judging from the evidences, the interior is extremely habitable! Vegetation in abundance; animals abound; the 'extinct' mammoth still lives! Byrd flew 1700 miles over the inner edge of the 'doughnut hole', and the Navy flew 2300 miles over the opposite inner edge. Both flights went a partial way into the inner Earth. And if this is all true, then no doubt extended flights to 10,000 miles and beyond have been made since 1957 into this hollow Earth, for we have the planes with the range to do it! If the government knew the significance of the Byrd-Navy flights, it would certainly not neglect to explore further.

"Alme Michel, in his 'straight line' theory, proved that most of the 'flight patterns' of the flying saucers are on a north-south course, which is exactly what would be true if the origin of the saucers is Polar.

"In the opinion of the editors of FLYING SAUCERS, this Polar origin of the flying saucers will now have to be factually disproved. It is completely necessary that this be done. More than a simple denial is necessary. Any denial must be accompanied with positive proof. FLYING SAUCERS suggests that such proof cannot be provided. FLYING SAUCERS takes the stand that all saucer groups should study the matter from the hollow Earth viewpoint, amass all confirmatory evidence available in the last two centuries, and search diligently for any contrary evidence. Now that we have tracked the saucers to the most logical origin (the one we have consistently insisted must exist because of the insurmountable obstacles of interstellar origin, which demands factors beyond imagination), that the saucers come from our own Earth, it must be proved or disproved, one way or the other.

"Why? Because if the interior of the Earth is populated by a highly scientific and advanced race, we must make profitable contact with them; and if they are mighty in their science, which includes the science of war, we must not make enemies of them; and if it is the intent of our governments to regard the interior of the Earth as 'virgin territory', and comparable to the 'Indian Territory' of North America when the settlers came over to take it away from its rightful owners, it is right of the people to know that intent, and to express their desire in the matter.

"The Flying Saucer has become the most important single fact in history. The answer to the questions raised in this article must be answered. Admiral Byrd has discovered a new and mysterious land, the center of the great unknown, and the most important discovery of all time. We have it from his own lips, from a man whose integrity has always been unimpeachable, and whose mind was one of the most brilliant of modern times.

"Let those who wish to call him a liar step forward and prove their claim! Flying saucers come from this Earth!"

So ends Ray Palmer's great article, "Saucers From the Earth!", which caused certain government secret agencies to confiscate the magazine and stop its distribution, so that it did not reach its 5000 subscribers. Why? Obviously because the government was convinced that such an unclaimed, unknown territory, vast in extent, exists and wished to be the first to claim it before the Russians did, and hence wanted all information about it to be kept secret. In his editorial of this memorable issue of "FLYING SAUCERS", its editor, Ray Palmer, wrote:

"In this issue we have presented the results of years of research, in which we advance the possibility that the saucers not only are from our own planet, and not from space, inner or outer, but that there is a tremendous mass of evidence to show that there is an UNKNOWN location of vast dimensions which is, insofar as we can safely state at this writing, also unexplored, where the saucers can, and most probably do originate. Even before the issue is off the press, one enterprising reader shoots the question at us: 'All right, if the saucers aren't from outer space, then how come Buck Nelson and a few dozen more claim to have ridden to Mars, Venus, the moon, etc.? Are you kidding us?'

"WE've read all the accounts of such voyages, and nowhere, in any of them, can we find positive evidence that space was traversed! In all of the accounts, we can see where the passengers could have been taken to this 'unknown land' discovered by Admiral Byrd, and if told they were on Mars, would not know the difference!

"It is a question, of course, whether Buck Nelson or anyone else, took a ride anywhere. We have only their word for it. We don't call them liars. We merely say that they can be deluded in many ways. To be specific, and we strongly suspect it, hypnosis can accomplish the trick...In another way, provided an actual trip in a saucer was made, the pilots of the saucers could have simulated a space trip (how high would it be necessary to go?) and instead taken their passengers to 'that mysterious land beyond the Pole', as Admiral Byrd called it.

"On September 15, 1959, the Soviet atomic powered icebreaker was launched and supposedly is on its way, or about to proceed, toward the North Pole with the intention of reaching it by smashing its way all the way through the ice. This would admittedly be quite an achievement, and more evidence of their amazing progress in science, but it is our opinion that the Russians do not do things merely for propaganda value."

In the January 15, 1960 issue of "THE SAUCERIAN BULLETIN", its editor, Gray Barker, writes:

"In the December issue of FLYING SAUCERS, Ray (Palmer) came out with his findings. We put the word 'new' in quotes above, for the theory had been advanced before, many years previously, in a book titled 'A Journey to the Earth's Interior, Or have The Poles Really Been Discovered?', now out of print and very rare. Many occult students, long before saucers became widely known about, believed that people lived inside the earth, emerging and entering through secret openings at the North and South Poles.

"Palmer presented only the first of his evidence in the December issue. It consisted of a review of newspaper and radio accounts of Admiral Richard E. Byrd's flight to the North Pole in 1947, the year the saucer reports got going, incidentally.

"In February of that year Byrd took off from an Arctic base and headed straight north to the Pole. Then Byrd kept flying north, beyond the Pole, and was amazed to discover iceless lands and lakes, mountains covered with trees, and even a monstrous animal moving through the underbrush below! For almost 1700 miles the plane flew over land, mountains, trees, lakes, rivers. After flying 1700 miles he was forced to turn back because of his gasoline supply limit for the return trip. So he retraced the flight back to the Arctic base.

"Not much was thought about the unusual flight at the time. We can't look up the reports, having no newspaper file handy, but Palmer has them.

"Palmer then instructs the reader to look at the globe. According to Byrd's reported flight, he shouldn't have seen anything but ice-covered ocean or partially-open water. Yet Byrd saw trees and other greenery. According to the globe, such a land just isn't there.

"Palmer next discusses similar geographical discrepancies at the South Pole, then draws the amazing conclusion:

"THE EARTH IS NOT SPHERICAL: INSTEAD IT IS SOMETHING LIKE A DOUGHNUT, Though perhaps not so flattened. At each pole there is a huge opening, so large that when one travels 'beyond' the pole, he actually enters the lip of the hole of the doughnut-shaped earth. If he traveled far enough he would travel through the 'hole' of the 'doughnut' and emerge at the other pole.

"Palmer further suggests that people live on the 'inside' of the earth, that such people emerge from the poles in flying saucers!

"He promises to present the remainder of his proofs later, but in the present issue of FLYING SAUCERS his case boils down to these main points:

"(1) Measurements of areas at the North and South Poles are larger than you can find room for on a map or globe, leading to the assumption such areas extend down into the 'doughnut'.

"(2) Some animals, particularly the musk-ox, migrate north in the wintertime, from the Arctic Circle. Foxes are found north of the 80th parallel, heading north, and appear well fed in a land where there is no food visible.

"(3) Arctic explorers agree it gets warmer as one heads north.

"(4) In the Arctic, coniferous trees drift ashore, from out of the north. Butterflies and bees are found in the far north, but never hundreds of miles south of that mount.

"(5)   Remains of mammoths, perfectly preserved, were found in Siberia, with the sparse food of the sub-Arctic region in its stomach. Such food could not have supported the animal. It must have come from the 'land beyond the Poles', Palmer postulates.

"(6)   Trouble with satelites shot over the South Pole bears out either the theory that land areas haven't been measured accurately, or the 'somebody' has been interfering with them."

In this connection it is interesting to note that U.S. newspapers, some time ago, published a report of a mysterious artificial satellite discovered to encircle the earth in an orbit that passed directly over both poles and which was sent by no known nation. Did it emerge from one of the poles and continue to rotate around the earth from its point of origin?

Gray Barker seems to agree with Palmer that saucers come from inside the Earth; and in his editorial quoted above, he asks: "What if there could be some unknown race, on some unexplored portion of the earth, which is responsible for the saucer?" Palmer's articles started me to thinking along that direction once again. THE INNER EARTH EXPLANATION WOULD FIT INTO MOST, IF NOT ALL THE FACETS OF THE SAUCER PICTURE.

"Various occult schools teach that polar entrances provide the doorways to cities such as Agharta Shamballah and others...Let us accept,for a moment, that such a people has existed inside the earth for thousands of years, even before man - or maybe they seeded the outside with man. Maybe they have constantly watched over him, and guided him, occasionally sending great teachers among him, occasionally assisting him with technology, giving rise to what we now call 'legends'. Maybe they built the Great Pyramid; maybe they are responsible for some of the 'miracles' reported in secular and religious histories...Until man, their protege, learned to be morally worthy, they would not wish to give him, suddenly, the knowledge of their existence of secrets of their technology.

"When man, however, invented the atomic bomb, the people of the inner earth would be greatly concerned about it. Maybe they would fear contamination which would reach them; maybe they would fear man could blow up the earth entirely; maybe they would be concerned only with man's own welfare.

"Halting, or controlling man's propensity for destruction would be a delicate problem, unless they would come out openly and inform him of their existence. Maybe they would figure they would eventually have to do so, and began a slow process of indoctrination, first merely letting him see the saucers flying around. When they learned man thought the saucers were from space; they pretend to be space people, 'contacting' him in their craft, and trying to indoctrinate him with peaceful philosophy (the reader will remember the majority of 'space people' have spoken out strongly against the Bomb).

"Maybe people like Albert K. Bender have figured out the obvious and the people of the inner earth have stopped them. It would indeed be frightening to face three men who could prove they were from the inside of the earth by being able to make some concrete demonstration of that fact."

"Those who have read my book will remember that before being
'hushed up', Bender, a New Zealand and an Australian saucer group
were charting the paths of saucers, with the idea of projecting
lines and determining the point of origin or rendezvous of the craft.
Bender told Harold Fulton of Civilian Saucer Investigation he believed
that saucers might be based in the Antarctic. F. Jarold, of the
Australian Flying Saucer Bureau, agreed with Bender, and suggested
they start what they would term 'Project X', concerned with charting
the paths of sightings.

"Right after that Bender clammed up, and Jarrold also complained
of a strange visitor shortly thereafter and abandoned saucer research
...Maybe the Government has known about the inner earth people for
some time and feel it necessary to keep the information away from us.
Maybe Bender was ready to break the story, and someone from the
government stepped in to prevent it."

That this is true is indicated by the fact that Dr. George Marlo,
director of the U.F.O. World Research, who claimed to have taken
many saucer trips to the earth's interior through the North Polar
opening, was visited by five FBI agents lately who warned him to
keep this matter hushed up and not talk too loudly about it, while
one of his members, Buck Nelson, who claimed to have taken a ride
on a flying saucer was visited by the same "three men in black" who
visited Bender.

ADMIRAL BYRD'S SOUTH POLAR FLIGHT

The following is quoted from "Rainbow City and Inner Earth
People" by Michael X:

"In the year 1947, Admiral Richard E. Byrd made a flight into
the South Polar region of the world. Before he started on the venture
Byrd made a mysterious statement:

"'I'd like to see that land BEYOND the Pole. That area beyond
the Pole is the center of the great unknown.'

"In the cockpit of his plane was a powerful, two-way radio.
When Byrd and his scientific companions took off from their base
at the South Pole, they managed to fly 1700 miles beyond it. That's
when the radio in Byrd's plane was put into use to report something
utterly incredible.

"There was a strange great valley below them. For some unknown
reason, the valley Byrd saw was not ice-covered as it should have
been in the frigid Antarctic. It was green and luxuriant. There
were mountains with thick forests of trees on them, there was lush
grass and underbrush. Most amazing, a huge animal was observed
moving through the underbrush. In a land of ice, snow and almost
perpetual 'deep-freeze'...here was a stupendous mystery.

"Byrd had discovered a strange great valley just beyond the
South Pole, where the weather temperature, believe it or not, was
something like 76 degrees!

"Both Alaska and Canada have had much more than their share of

62

sightings (of flying saucers) in recent months. Why? Is there some
connection with the 'land beyond the Pole' - that Unknown Country
which we suspect is nothing less than THE INNER EARTH itself?

"Indeed there is a connection. If the saucers enter and leave
the Inner Earth by way of the polar entrances, quite naturally they'd
be seen by Alaskans and Canadians much more frequently than they
would by people in other parts of the world. Alaska is close to the
North Pole. So is Canada.

"When Admiral Byrd went into the Unknown Country, into the
center of the great unknown, where was he? If Marshall Gardner
were here now I'm sure he'd agree with us when we gently suggest
that Byrd was at the very doorway of the inner earth. In the South
Pole area it lies beyond the Pole...in Eastern Antarctica, that
fabulous region never before seen by man'.

"In February of 1947, a most remarkable discovery was made in
the continent of Antarctica. This discovery is known now as 'Bunger's
Oasis'. Lt. Commander David Bunger was at the controls of one of
the six large transport planes used by Admiral Byrd for the U.S.
Navy's 'Operation Highjump' (1946-1947).

"Bunger was flying inland from the Shackleton Ice Shelf, near
Queen Mary Coast of Wilkes Land. He and his crew were about four
miles from the coastline where open water lies.

"For two months previous to this moment, all that Bunger and
his flight crew had seen below was white polar wasteland. In one
dramatic second all that monotony vanished. Suddenly they could see
a large dark spot of land up ahead of them...an area some three
hundred square miles in size. It seemed to be completely free of
snow or ice. And it had many lakes.

"The land itself was ice-free. The lakes were of many different
colors, ranging from rusty red, green, to deep blue. The strange
thing about the colors is that they were bright, as though something
in the water caused them to attract more light. Each of the lakes
was more than three miles long. The water was warmer than the ocean,
as Bunger soon found by landing his seaplane on one of the lakes.
Each lake had a gently sloping beach.

"Around the four edges of the Oasis, which was roughly square
in shape, Bunger saw endless and eternal white snow and ice. Two
sides of the Oasis rose nearly one hundred feet high, and consisted
of great ice walls. The other two sides had a more gradual and
gentle slope."

This would indicate warmer conditions, as would exist if one
entered into the South Polar opening, leading to the earth's interior.
Otherwise one cannot explain the existence of such an Oasis of
unfrozen territory, which was not the result of hot volcanic activity
beneath the surface of the land, which covers three hundred square
miles and is too big an area to be affected by volcanic heat supply.
Warm currents from the earth's interior could account for this."

In January 1955, at a four day conference of the Brazilian
Theosophical Society, in Rio de Janeiro; Paulo J. Strauss, a Commander

of the Brazilian Navy, said: "One should not ignore the legends of enchanted cities...I believe these mysterious apparatuses (flying saucers) come from the center of the earth, where it has long been believed that life exists to a degree far advanced over our own civilization." This is the opinion of Prof. Henrique de Souza, president of the Brazilian Theosophical Society, a noted esotericist and archeologist. Strauss also believes that Colonel Fawcett is still alive with his son Jack, dwelling in a subterranean city of the Atlanteans which he reached through entering a tunnel opening in Roncador Mountains of Northeast Matto Grosso. This is also the opinion of Prof. de Souza and his Theosophical students, who have a large temple in Sao Lourenzoa, State of Minas Gerais, Brazil, dedicated to Agharta, the Subterranean World.

It is claimed that there once existed an advanced civilization on the prehistoric continent of Atlantis, whose scientific development was beyond our own, and that their air vehicles, known as "vimanas", were identical with what we now call flying saucers. This great civilization destroyed itself through a terrible nuclear war which brought on a terrible geological catastrophe and a flood. Prior to its total destruction, certain better inhabitants of Atlantis escaped by flying in their flying saucers into the hollow interior of the earth through the polar openings, where they continued to live ever since. These Atlanteans are a race of giants; and their final war is referred to in mythology as the War of the Titans. Michael X writes:

"I believe that Atlantis was every bit real, and that the Atlanteans' ancestors are living today, now, in the interior of the earth. They are in all probability very large people, physically. Perhaps blonde giants. But why believe they are still in existence?

"Because persistent rumors have it that a vast system of subterranean TUNNELS exist beneath the land of South America. Secret openings are said to exist, leading from the surface of the earth into the tunnels. In his book 'Agharta', Robert E. Dickhoff claims that a fantastic network of tunnels exists underground...According to Dickhoff, one tunnel surfaces in the Matto Grosso region of Brazil, precisely where Col. Fawcett vanished in 1925!...Perhaps he found the 'secret city'..and more. A tunnel nearby leading down into the earth's fantastic cavern kingdoms, and maybe the people there never permitted him to leave." (This is the opinion of Commander Paulo J. Strauss and Prof. H.J. de Souza.)

We quote from a letter from Ottmar Kaub: Writing about the book, "The Smoky God", by Willis George Emerson, he says: "This book has the books of Reed and Gardner all beat. I read it through at one sitting and was never so excited in my life. The Smoky God is the inner sun. It is supposed to be the true story of a Norse father and son who, with their small fishing boat and unbounded courage, attempted to find the land beyond the North Wind as they had heard of its warmth and beauty. A miraculous storm and wind carried themmost of the distance. They spent two years there and returned via the South Pole and the father lost his life when a berg broke in two and destroyed the boat. The son was rescued and subsequently spent 24 years in prison for insanity when he told the true story. When he was released, he told the story to no one, but after 26 years as a fisherman, he saved enough to retire in this country, coming to

Illinois and then to California. In his nineties, by accident, the novelist, Willis George Emerson, befriended him and was told the story; on the old man's deathbed he relinquished the maps that he had made of the Inner Earth and the manuscript. He refused to take chances while he lived, due to his past experience in having people disbelieve him and consider him insane to mention it.

"Olaf Jansen claims that the four rivers of Genesis (Paradise) are very large and flowing in the Inner Earth, and much gold was there as Genesis states. The rivers are larger than the Amazon. Jansen checked all the explorers, as Reed and Gardner did later on, and Emerson has this material quoted briefly, but proves all the points about the Inner Earth. The 'Smoky God' is a masterpiece based on Arctic reports..."

Michael X, in his book referred to above, quotes Dr. Nephi Cottam of Los Angeles, who said that one of his patients, a man of Nordic descent, told him the following story:

"I live near the Arctic Circle in Norway. One summer my friend and I made up our minds to take a boat trip together, and go as far as we could into the North country. So we put one month's food provisions into a small fishing boat and with sail and also a good engine in our boat, set out to sea.

"At the end of one month we had traveled far into the north, beyond the pole and into a strange new country. We were much astonished at the weather there. Warm, and at times at night it was almost too warm to sleep. Then we saw something so strange we both were astonished. Ahead of the warm, open sea we were on, was what looked like a great mountain. Into that mountain at a certain point, the ocean seemed to be emptying. Mystified, we continued in that direction and found ourselves sailing into a vast canyon leading into the interior of the earth. We kept sailing and then saw what surprised us - a sun shining into the earth!

"The ocean that had carried us into the hollow interior of the earth gradually became a river. This river leads, as we came to realize later...all through the inner surface of the world from one end to the other. It can take you, if you follow it long enough, from the North Pole clear through to the South Pole.

"We saw that the inner earth's surface was divided, even as the outer one is, into both land and water. There is plenty of sunshine, and both animal and vegetable life abound there. We sailed further and further into this fantastic country...fantastic because everything was huge in size as compared with things on the outside. Plants are big, trees gigantic, and then we came upon the GIANTS.

"They were dwelling in homes and towns, just as we do on the earth's surface. And they used a type of electrical conveyance like a mono-rail car, to transport people. It ran along the river's edge from town to town.

"Several of the inner earth inhabitants - huge giants - detected our boat on the river, and were quite amazed. They seemed just as astonished to see us as we were to see them! They were, however, quite friendly. We were invited to dine with them in their homes, and so my companion and I separated - he going with one giant to that giant's home, and I going with another giant to his home.

"My gigantic friend brought me home to his family, and I was completely dismayed to see the huge size of all the objects in his home. The dinner table was collosal. A plate was put before me and filled with a portion of food so big it would have fed me abundantly for an entire week! The giant offered me a cluster of grapes and each grape was as big as one of our outer-earth peaches. I tasted one and found it far sweeter than any I had ever tasted 'outside'. In the inner earth all the fruits and vegetables taste far better and more flavorsome than those we have on the outer earth.

"We stayed with the giants for one year, enjoying their companionship as much as they enjoyed knowing us. We observed many strange and unusual things during our visit with these remarkable people, and were continually amazed at their scientific progress and inventions. All of this time they were never unfriendly to us, and we were allowed to return to our own home in the same manner in which we had come - in fact, they courteously offered their protection if we should need it for the return voyage."

Dr. George Marlo claims to have made this same trip many times by flying saucer, and has met the people living inside the earth's crust and is known to them. He described the people as being 12 to 14 feet tall. The men have short beards. He speaks of choirs of 25,000 people. The men wear sandles and shorts. He speaks of musical instruments, especially harps. He speaks of grapes as large as oranges and apples the size of a man's head. He mentions five cities, named Eden, Nigi, Delfi, Jehu and Hectea. They speak a language like Sanscrit (probably Atlantean). He said they marry at the age of 75 to 100 and live for 600 to 800 years of age. He speaks of birds with 30 foot wingspread, which lay eggs two feet long. He mentions tortoises 25 to 30 feet long, and elephant-like creatures (resembling those which emerged from the North Polar opening to be frozen as mammoths); and penguins 9 feet tall. He speaks of trees 1,000 feet tall and 120 feet in diameter. He said that the compass inside the earth points north and leads one to the South Polar opening.

ARGUMENTS OF MARSHALL B. GARDNER IN FAVOR OF THE
THEORY THAT THE EARTH IS HOLLOW

Marshall B. Gardner wrote his book, "A JOURNEY TO THE EARTH'S INTERIOR or HAVE THE POLES REALLY BEEN DISCOVERED?" in 1913, in which he defends his belief in a hollow, rather than a solid, earth as follows:

"Our theory may be untrue, but if it is, then the findings of Nansen and every other Arctic explorer, of Sir Robert Ball, Percival Lowell and every other astronomer, are wrong. For upon the work done by these men and upon no other considerations whatsoever than those of pure scientific knowledge are the ideas of this book built.

"Now as a matter of fact the scientists themselves no longer hold the ideas about the constitution of the earth that were taught in all text books only a few years ago. The notion that the earth is a great ball of material which has hardened into a shell or crust on the outside, but which is full of molten material within, getting hotter and hotter as we reach the center - that notion <u>is now no longer generally held</u>. And no other theory has quite taken its place.

"Some think that while the earth may have a solid center that it does have a liquid center somewhere between its center and its surface. But none of the theories up to the present have explained all the facts.

"Of course it is very easy for anyone to deny all the facts of science and get up some purely private explanation of the formation of the earth. The man who does that is a crank...There is one man who has stated that the earth is an immense hollow sphere and that mankind and the land and oceans and even the stars are all on the inside of it! But he is a crank for he has simply taken his private notion, evolved within his own brain and has made a religion of it. (Note: Dr. Cyrus R. Teed, M.D., known as 'Koresh', startled the world and his followers with this strange theory in the early 1920's - R.B.)

"We take the opposite course. We begin with the facts. We claim that the earth is a HOLLOW BODY with an immense opening at each polar axis - an opening about 1400 miles in diameter - and that there is in the interior of the earth a sun which warms it and gives it light. We state that this formation of a hollow shell around a central sun, with polar openings, is not alone the formation of the earth but of every planetary body throughout the stellar universe. Why do we say that? Because we think it ought to be? Because we wish to impose our own idea on to the facts? No, but because we can see these polar openings and occasionally the gleam of the central sun as we look at Mars or Venus through a telescope."

Michael X comments as follows on Gardner's statements: "A hollow earth? Why not? The idea isn't too surprising, and some of the evidence I shall include in this report is astonishing. The big thing, the really important thing is - If the earth is hollow it may well be inhabited. By whom? Living beings, human and otherwise! Frankly, from what we've seen, heard and added-up in our mind in recent months, we believe the inner earth is not only inhabited by humans, but by humans far more ADVANCED IN SCIENCE THAN WE ARE! And that poses a very serious problem.

"Imagine a race of fellow human beings dwelling far beneath the surface of this earth, in a vast hollow interior region some 4,400 miles in circumference. Figuring four directions, that is a lot of land area. Population of the 'Inner Earth' could be as large, maybe larger than that of our outer earth.

"Now suppose that race of people inside the earth are 500 to 1,000 years ahead of our nations in inventions. If that were true, they'd have already perfected the kind of flying craft that are most efficient - FLYING SAUCERS. And suppose they decided to 'investigate' the outer earth where you and I are living. They'd come up through secret opinions at the poles and elsewhere, in their flying craft and we'd see in our skies FLYING SAUCERS FROM INNER EARTH!"

Now it is remarkable that identical ideas should come to independent writers in different parts of the world, who had no connection with each other. While Michael X wrote the above in the United States, down in Brazil a writer named Huguenin wrote a book, "FLYING SAUCERS: FROM THE SUBTERRANEAN WORLD TO THE SKY"; and while Marshall B. Gardner and William Reed wrote their books to prove that the Earth is hollow, down in Brazil, many years ago, a rare unknown book was written by one of the first German settlers, in Old German, to which we previously referred, based on Atlantean traditions preserved among the Indians, who passed it on to this German, to the effect that the Earth has a hollow interior and a central sun, and in the inside lives a super race that composes a civilization far in advance of our own. The only difference was that this book spoke of access to this world being achieved through certain tunnels that open in Santa Catarina and Parana states of Brazil, which are the parts of the world where contact between the interior and the exterior world may be most easily affected, while Gardner's and Reed's books spoke of the polar region being the place where contact between the two worlds may be had.

It is a well known fact that while the South Polar region is constantly accumulating ice at a terrific speed, causing the frozen continent of Antarctics to steadily increase in size and weight, on the other hand, the North Polar ice cap seems to be melting, causing icebergs to break loose and drift southward in greater amount than ever before. Some believe that ever since the commencement of the Atomic Era there has been a steady increase in the temperature at the North Pole, causing ice to melt, and of the Northern Hemisphere in general. Perhaps the accumulation of radioactive fallout particles in the stratosphere, troposphere and atmosphere of the North Temperate Zone, especially within the "Fallout Band" between the 30th and 60th parallel, accounts for this.

Now this would mean that the opening at the North Pole would be easier of access and less impeded by ice than that of the South Pole. It is interesting to note that while there is soil found in the North Polar area, in the Antarctic there is only ocean water and ice two miles thick. It is also interesting to note that while there are Northern Lights, there are no "Southern" Lights. Could this be due to the fact that while the central sun is able to send its rays through the more open North Polar opening, to project on the night sky, the South Polar opening is blocked by ice, so that its rays cannot emerge from there? But if the openings are as large as Gardner and Reed postulate, this could hardly be possible, since an opening so large could not possibly be blocked up by ice.

However, if the ancestors of the Eskimos, as well as polar animals, as seals and bears, also mammoths and prehistoric elephant-like tropical animals, living or in form of their remains are found in the Arctic region and not in the Antarctic, and if they all come from the Inner Earth, then it would indicate that contact between the Inner Earth and the outer surface is more easily effected at the North Pole than at the South Pole, where the only fauna to be found are penguins.

The rhythmic ebb and flow of ocean tides has been attributed to lunar magnetism since tides rise and fall in harmony when the moon passes through its phases. But in the case of ocean waves, it is

68

different, since they follow a rhythmic cycle that has no relation to the moon's phases. We believe that the ocean waters continually circulate around, passing through the hollow interior of the earth, coming out at one polar opening and then; after completing the cycle, entering through the other polar opening, thus maintaining a continual circulation, and that it is the combination of this circulatory movement and the earth's rotation on its axis that causes the phenomenon of ocean waves - for if the oceans were stationary bodies of water, like lakes, they would have no waves. It is the combination of these movements that results in a rocking, back-and-forth undulation of ocean waters, which produce the common, yet strange, phenomenon of ocean waves,

THE AGHARTAN ORDER AND EXPEDITION

Prior to the sinking of Atlantis, a group of wise and good Atlanteans, who had foreknowledge of the catastrophe, came to Brazil and constructed here subterranean refuges in the form of underground cities, connected with each other by tunnels, where they established residence prior to the outbreak of the nuclear war that brought on the flood that sank Atlantis. In their new subterranean home these Atlanteans were able to survive the universal destruction of life on the Earth's surface caused by the radioactive poisoning of the atmosphere that this nuclear war produced.

Incredible as it may seem, there is evidence that Atlanteans still live in underground cities under Brazil, especially in the states of Santa Cartarina, Parana and Matto Grosso. After some years of research the writer is convinced of this fact and also that contacting them will be our last hope of survival if and when a nuclear war breaks out. For this reason he has organized the Aghartan Expedition for the purpose of investigating eight different tunnels he knows in Santa Catarina and Parana, with the hope of reaching the subterranean cities to which they may lead, and then establishing cordial relations with the subterranean Atlanteans for the purpose of bringing qualified surface inhabitants to their subterranean cities.

The purpose of the Aghartan Order is to prepare and gather such potential survivors, who will come to Santa Catarina and will settle here until they are invited to the subterranean cities.

COSMOLOGICAL EVIDENCE IN FAVOR OF A HOLLOW EARTH

Marshall B. Gardner, in his 450 page work, "A Journey to the Earth's Interior or Have the Poles Really Been Discovered?", presents the following argument in defense of his theory of a hollow earth and a central sun. In the natural condensation of solar systems out of nebulae, the centriful force of the rotation of each of the planets that separate from the central mass would tend to cause the heavier constituents to be thrown out to their periphery, leaving a hollow center.

Also, just as, in the formation of the solar system, some of the original fire remained at the center to form the sun, so, in the case of each individual planet, by the same process by which the solar system as a whole was formed, and by a continuation of the same general movement of rotation and the centriful throwing out of the heavier masses to the periphery (as shown by the fact that the most outermost planets, as Uranus and Neptune, are much larger than those nearer the sun, as Mercury and Venus), in the case of each of the planets, in their formation, some of the original fire remains in the center of each, to form the central sun, while their heavier constituents are thrown toward their surface to form the solid crust, while the center is left hollow.

In addition, due to the rotary motion, the crust of each planet forms a polar depression leading to the hollow interior, rather than being perfectly round with a hole at the poles.

It is Gardner's theory that all planets are hollow and have a central sun, this being the basic pattern according to which solar systems are formed from the primordial nebula from which they originate. Also, our universe must have a central sun too, around which the stars circulate - the Sun Behind the Sun of occult traditions.

"THE SMOKY GOD": THE CENTRAL SUN

Ottmar Kaub, who has helped greatly by summarizing Reed's and Gardner's books for us, sent us a bibliography of the works that Gardner consulted before writing his book, which we are giving at the end, to prove his theory that the earth is hollow with openings at the poles and with a central sun. This evidence comes chiefly from Arctic explorers. Kaub then comments:

"Now that we have presented the bibliography of Marshall B. Gardner, we notice the absence of two books, one of which would have made Gardener jump out of his skin. What a pity he was not acquainted with them. One is "The Smoky God", which title refers to the Central Sun, which some Inner Earth inhabitants say is the home of God. It was published in 1908 and Gardner could have heard of it, but obviously he did not. The book is by Willis George Emerson. It is the true story of Olaf Jansen and his father, hardy fishermen who sailed their small fishing boat into the Inner Earth, remained there for two years, met the people and learned the language and then sailed out again through the South Polar opening, after which Olaf Jansen left his story to the world. It is too thrilling to summarize and must be left for you to read when it is republished.

"The other book is by William F. Warren. We do not have the date. The title is 'Paradise Found, or the Cradle of the Human Race at the North Pole'. The author just barely missed the true shape of the earth, but was right about the location of Paradise. Olaf Jansen claims he saw the four rivers of the Garden of Eden in the Inner Earth, which is the true Eden. Olaf Jansen said that the people inside the earth live from 400 to 800 years and are highly advanced in science, sending their thoughts through the air by certain types of radiations and have sources of power better than out electricity. Olaf Jansen spent 28 years in prison because he tried to bring this truth to the world.

"Olaf Jansen lived to be 96 on this horrid Outer Earth. There are 186 pages. There are eleven beautiful illustrations made by some artist (John A. Williams), but no clue to his address. The picture of the Central Sun is very good. The men are twelve or more feet high and wear knee breaches, and have short beards. They use gold generally in decorations.

In a letter to "Flying Saucers" magazine, Wm. L. Constantine writes:

"For many years it has been my opinion that a race of highly intelligent people do actually live in the earth's core. If Admiral Byrd did find this 74 degree climate at the pole in 1947, is it not a more than reasonable assumption that our government would make a great effort to follow through? Byrd says he was forced to turn back after 2300 miles because of a dwindling gas supply. Granting this to be true, this problem no longer exists. If my information is correct, we have planes that can do far better now. I believe this has already been done and that landings have been made and contacts firmly established on a sound and lasting understanding.

"Can it be that our government is trying to lull the rest of the world?"

INNER EARTH PEOPLE AND FLYING SAUCERS

The following are reports told the writer in Brazil concerning Inner Earth people and flying saucers. There is no proof at all that these reports are true. They may be lies invented by the narrators in order to create an impression. But whether true or false they are interesting and show along what lines people are thinking today.

A Russian who formerly served in the Russian army said he and his troops once reached Lhasa, Tibet, where he was stationed some time, and there he came in touch with a secret society of Tibetan vegetarians who made regular trips by flying saucer through the North Polar opening to the hollow interior of the earth. He says he saw the saucer that made these trips. He said that the supreme object of all Tibetan lamas and yogis is to prepare their bodies to be worthy to be picked up by a flying saucer and carried to the hollow interior of the earth, whose human population consists mostly of Tibetan lamas and Oriental yogis, with very few Westerners, since Westerners are too bound to the things of this world, while lamas and yogis wish to escape from this miserable world and enter a much better world in the hollow interior of the earth.

The reason why subterranean people sent their flying saucers to us after the Hiroshima atomic explosion in 1945 was because they were afraid that further explosions might poison the air that comes into their interior atmosphere through the polar openings, coming from the outer air. Since inhabitants of other planets would have nothing to worry about if we poisoned our atmosphere by nuclear explosions, while inhabitants of the earth's interior, who receive their air from the outside atmosphere would have plenty to worry about, it is clear that flying saucers do not come from other planets but from the hollow interior of the earth.

This contactee describes flying saucers as made of a brilliant nickel that glows with a light at night. He says that the people of the earth's interior wield a form of energy beyond atomic energy (electromagnetism) which motivates their flying saucers. They use this superior energy (the "vril" of Bulwer Lytton) only for peaceful purposes.

Also these people have one government and one nation and are not divided into warring nations as we are. This is helped by their speaking all the same language. They are in advance of us in all ways. They live without religion as we know it, obeying the laws of nature, which they consider better than believing in religion and supernatural gods and saviors, while disobeying nature's laws in our daily lives, such as by eating meat, indulging in sex, etc. These people are vegetarians and all live in complete chastity.

According to this contactee, all flying saucers emerge from the South Polar opening and tend to fly in the direction of the North Polar opening, entering there. It is claimed that ocean water circulates around the earth in the same manner, passing from the outside oceans through a polar opening to the inside oceans, and then flying to the other polar opening and leaving from there to reappear on the surface. This circulation of ocean water plus the earth's rotations produce the phenomenon of ocean waves, even if the moon is responsible for ocean tides.

The above explains that observed tendency of flying saucers to fly in pole-to-pole directions. A saucer seen in the Amazon was claimed to come from the south. Many observations of saucers were made in the Antarctic and were referred to as the "Antarctic Mystery", leading some to think there is a saucer base there.

MYSTERIES OF THE PYRAMID OF GIZEH

Robert Dickhoff, in his book "Agharta", mentions that the secret chambers of the Pyramid of Gizeh were connected by tunnels with the Subterranean world. An Egyptian informant says that at the base of this pyramid are three tunnels that radiate in different directions. Two lead to dead ends, but the third seems to go on and on and may have once connected Atlantis with its colony in Egypt by passing under the Mediterranean and Atlantic. Two Swedes tried to traverse this long tunnel till its end and never returned. While believed to have died, rescue parties could not find them. This caused the government to forbid anyone from entering this third long tunnel, though they were permitted to enter the other two. There are strange reports of ancient Egyptians (or Atlanteans?) having been seen inside the long tunnel, coming from the Subterranean World. Many believe that the Swedes who disappeared joined these people. A popular book was selling in Egypt some time ago entitled "THE MYSTERIOUS PATH TO THE UNKNOWN WORLD", dealing with the apparently endless third tunnel below the Pyramid of Gizeh and the world to which it leads.

Atlantis was connected by suboceanic tunnels with its Egyptian colony to the east and its Brazilian and Inca colony to the west. It is probable that the real purpose of the pyramids was not to serve as tombs for the dead kinds but as covered entrances of tunnels connecting Egypt with the Subterranean World and so built to prevent

the entry of flood waters, since their builders had foreknowledge of
the flood waters, since their builders had foreknowledge of the flood
that would occur and cause the sinking of Atlantis. The floodwaters
would have to rise to the top of the pyramids to enter the subterranean chambers and tunnels below. Since Egypt is flat low country,
pyramids were necessary for this purchase, like in Yucatan, whereas
in mountainous country and in high plateaus, as in Brazil, no pyramids
are needed as tunnels here open on mountain tops which provide natural
protection against the entry of water during floods.

As Donnelly points out in his book "Atlantis the Antediluvian
World", the pyramids, with their four sides and truncated top,
memorialize the sacred mountain of the gods in the center of Atlantis,
from where their builders came. It is probably that messengers from
the Subterranean gods traveled on swift-moving vehicles through the
tunnels that open at the base of the pyramids.

A report has been circulating that some scientists entered a
tunnel in West Africa that run under the ocean bed in the direction
of the vanished Atlantis, which was finally reached and many mechanical contrivances were their seen on the ocean bed, including motor
vehicles. How true this report is, the writer cannot say. Another
report refers to the discovery of a subterranean city by Brazilian
scientists, reached by a tunnel opening near the border of the states
of Santa Catarina and Parana. Similar subterranean cities were
reported in Matto Grosso, whose entrances are guarded by fierce
Chavantes and Bat Indians.

AVIATOR PHOTOGRAPHS A GREEN VALLEY BEYOND THE NORTH POLE

A Canadian correspondent wrote us (June 18, 1960):

"Some time ago 'The Globe and Mail' of Toronto published a
photo taken of a green valley up in the North Pole region. Evidently
the pilot took the picture from the air but did not attempt to land.
I saved the picture and have it some place cut out from the newspaper. It was a very nice valley and contained rolling green hills."

Obviously this was the same kind of warm country beyond the
Pole that Admiral Byrd visited when he flew 2300 miles beyond. This
photograph confirms what Byrda reported that he saw.

ARE ALL PLANETS HOLLOW WITH CENTRAL SUNS?
Astronomical Evidence in Favor of a Hollow Earth

Mr. Ottmar Kaub, who supplied us with the summaries of Reed's
and Gardner's books, rare copies of which he found in a library,
wrote:

"Gardner's book is too thick to summarize. His book contains
all the information in the book by Reed, but he does add a few
points, especially from astronomy, that should be given special
consideration. On page 29 he quotes Professor Lowell, the astronomer,
as stating that he has seen gleams of light coming from the polar
cap of Mars. (According to Gardner, this is due to rays from the

73

central sun of Mars passing through the polar opening.) Similar
bright streamers of light have been observed coming from the polar
region of Venus. During a transit of Mercury across the sun, the
planet of course is black on the side toward us, and yet one astronomer, prior to 1920, had observed a bright light comparable to the
light of our sun, coming from the black disc of Mercury.

"Gardner concludes that these planets also are hollow, have
large openings which are misnamed polar caps of ice and snow, but in
reality are white due to the large amount of fog or clouds in those
regions, and that openings in the fog or clouds permit the bright
central sun to shine through, and such bright light has repeatedly
been observed by astronomers, who, not guessing the truth, were not
able to offer any satisfactory explanation. Gardner claims that at
times these polar caps disappear suddenly, due to a change of
weather. Ice and snow could not melt so rapidly."

THE CIRCULAR POLAR CAP OF MARS AND VENUS

We quote from Marshall B. Gardner:

"In appearance Mars is a reddish planet to the naked eye, but
the telescope reveals a surface of variegated color. There are many
dark patches in the surface and they are fixed - but at each pole is
a large circular white cap which diminishes in size in the spring
season until it sometimes disappears totally. But the reader should
not jump to the conclusion that this diminishing in spring indicates
that the cap is composed of snow or ice. The astronomers themselves
have begun to doubt that. For the cap does not diminish gradually
as it would if it were gradually melting ice. It does it by sudden
jumps.

"Mr. Mounder quotes Professor Newcomb as remarking: 'There is
no evidence that snow like ours is ever formed around the poles of
Mars. It does not seem possible that any considerable fall of such
snow could take place, nor is there any necessity of supposing
actual snow or ice to account for the white caps.'

", the astronomers who try to theorize on the basis of polar
snow caps are simply getting themselves into logical trouble.

"In his book entitled 'Mars', Lowell says, in presenting a
map of what he thinks is the ICE CAP of the southern Martian pole:

" 'It will be seen from it how much farther advanced is our
knowledge of either of our own.'

"What a significant admission that is, and not so much out of
date at the present time as most people imagine who have taken all
their knowledge of our earthly poles at second hand and never exam-
ined into it.

"An English astronomer, E.S.Crew, in his text book, 'The Growth
of a Planet', remarks that polar conditions on earth and on Mars
cannot be compared because the meteorological conditions are quite
different in the two planets.

"But supposing that what we see can be explained only by conditions which are not meteological? Then the two planets, perhaps, can be compared. It is because our theory points to something permanent in the structure of the planet as the explanation of polar phenomena, and not to mere meteorological changes, that we can compare the two planets and show similar agencies at work on each of them, testifying to a structure which is the same in the one as in the other - and as all others indeed.

"But let us turn to the observation of Professor Lowell of the utmost value. On page 86 of his book, 'Mars', Professor Lowell records:

'Meanwhile an interesting phenomenon occurred in the cap on June 7 (this was in 1894). On that morning at about a quarter to six, as I was watching the planet, I saw suddenly two points like stars flash out in the midst of the polar cap. Dazzlingly bright upon the duller background of the snow, these stars shone for a few moments and then slowly disappeared. The seeing at the time was very good. It is at once evident that the other-world apparitions were not the fabled lights of the Martian folk, but the glint of ice slopes flashing for a moment earthward as the rotation of the planet turned the slope to the proper angle, though no intelligence lay behind the action of the lights, being Nature's own flash lights.'

"These star-like points had, however, been seen before, and Lowell goes on to check up his observations with those of others.

"'Calculation showed the position of the star points to be in longitude 280 degrees and 290 degrees, and in latitude 76 degrees south. At this place on the planet then there was a range of slopes sufficiently tilted to reflect the sun from their ice-clad sides. On comparing its position with Green's map of his observations upon the caps of Maderia in 1877, it appeared that this was the identical position of spot where he had seen star-points then, and where Mitchell had seen them in 1846, to whom they had suggested the same conclusion.'

"Now it is important in the above, to note exactly what was seen - far more important, to do that than to pass it over and listen to Lowell's ideas, merely, about what he saw. And the definite thing that Lowell plainly saw, and was astonished by, and specifically mentioned, was 'two points like stars flash out in the midst of the polar cap.'

"And let us also note that Green saw, many years earlier, two spots and that Mitchell saw, as far back as 1846, something similar but with a difference-which we shall come to presently. But meanwhile let us see how inadequate is Professor Lowell's explanation of what he saw---so that we may keep distinct the actual thing and the mere theory which was made up to account for it.

"In the first place, Edward S. Morse, in his 'MARS AND ITS MYSTERY', a book which warmly supports Lowell's theories about life on Mars, on page 138 tells of photographs taken by Professor Pickering of the polar regions of Mars in which a vast area of white appeared around the pole in the _amazingly short space of twenty-four hours_. In that time an area as large as the United States was visible as a white cap, and then it gradually disappeared."

"And yet Professor Lowell asks us to believe---if this is really ice at the poles---that it is so permanent that two very steep slopes---so steep as to reflect light direct to Earth---should keep their size and shape and positions from 1846, when Mitchell saw them, until the present day. And we remember, also, Professor Newcomb's explanation that there is no snow or ice at the Martian poles but only immensely fine hoar frost---which could not possibly pile up into steep cliffs and reflect light to us in the way described. And even Professor Lowell himself, in his other book, 'Mars As the Abode of Life', admits that it would be very hard to prove that the polar caps were composed of snow or hoar frost, and that he could not have, to his satisfaction, proved it if it had not been that around the polar area was to be seen a band of dark blue which he took to be water from the melting ice or the snow cap. But later on in the same book he speaks (page 140) of the well known total disappearance of the one cap and the almost entire extinction of the other, showing how each summer melts what the winter had deposited, and that in both cases that is nearly the sum total of the cap.

"But if both caps are thus depleted by each summer, how could a great ice cliff--again we ask the same question--remain since 1846 to reflect to us the light that Lowell saw?"

Kaub comments: "The band of dark blue is the rim of the curve as one would travel from Outer Mars to Inner Mars, the blue band being water---the while cap being clouds and fog---which lifts here and there at times allowing the bright inner sun to shine thru. The disappearance of the white caps 'by sudden jumps' is caused by sudden changes in weather, very similar to what we are all familiar with on our own Earth. Now my comment: The reason that this band of water would be darker than other ocean water is that as the rim curves very much as the Inner Mars is approached, less light of the solar sun reaches it, and as yet none of the central sun. One would have to be inside of Mars to receive any benefit from the central sun of Mars. We now continue with Gardner:

"No there are too many contradictions there. Ice cliffs, if they formed in the polar regions of Mars, would form at so many different angles and in so many different relative positions that flashes would be constantly sent over to us. There would be a display as continuous as that of heliograph signaling. As a matter of fact, what Lowell really did see was a direct beam--two direct beams at the same moment--flashing from the central sun of Mars out through the aperture of the Martian pole. Does not the blue rim around that area to which Lowell has referred indicate the optical appearance of the reflecting surface of the planet gradually curving over to the interior so that at a certain part of the curve it begins to cease reflecting the light? And the fact that is not seen often simply shows that it is only when Mars is in a certain position with relation to the earth that we are able to penetrate the mouth of the polar opening and catch the direct beam."

BEAM OF LIGHT WAS YELLOW

"That it was a direct beam of light that Lowell saw, and not mere reflection may easily be proved. He particularly said, in writing about his discovery, that the light from the Martian cap was yellow when it was viewed at night. What does that imply?

"The reader can best answer that after making a simple observation. Let him go out any night and look into a lighted window from a distance. The flood of light coming from the window will be yellow. The reader will also find that all artists paint lighted windows even through the night as being yellow. We may go close up to the window and see that the source of the light is an incandescent electric light bulb which may be dazzlingly white and yet the light at a little distance is just as yellow as if the window were illuminated with yellow flamed candles.

"Also, the reader may try something else. Let him after looking at the window from a short distance as we have suggested, move away to one side, so that he no longer looks directly into the window, but sees it from a very great angle. The light from the window will then be seen to extend out beyond the window to a certain extent.

"We may now apply this to Mars. It proves that the light from the polar region of Mars is a direct illuminant from within the planet, because that light, seen at night, is yellow. Any other sort of light, a reflection from a snowy surface, for instance, or a reflection from sand or mountain surfaces, would be white."

At this point of the book we see eight photographs of Mars thru a telescope with this comment underneath;-'Views of Mars taken at the Yerkes Observatory Sept. 28, 1902, showing the white circle or so-called snow-cap, projected beyond the planet's surface, which precludes all possibility of its being snow or ice.'

"And if the reader will refer to our photograph of Mars on page 80 he will notice that the light from the polar opening extends in a spreading mist of luminosity of a very definite from which cannot be mistaken and which is obviously many miles above the surface of the planet. Now let the reader compare that with what he saw when he looked through the night at a lighted window at an angle, it is the same sort of extension of light. So that again proves that the Martian light is coming from a direct source and illuminating the section of the Martian atmosphere just above the polar opening."

BRILLIANT LIGHT FROM POLAR CAPS

"Mitchell, whom Lowell quotes in the above extract, has some very interesting points to make. He speaks of the brilliant light of the polar caps--a light more brilliant than that of the other surfaces which are supposed to be covered with ice. Then comes his description of the beam of light which we hold to come direct from the central sun of Mars; 'On the evening of the 30th of August 1845, I observed, for the first time, a small bright spot, nearly or quite round, projecting out of the lower side of the polar spot. In the early part of the evening the small bright spot seemed to be partly buried in the large one. After the lapse of an hour or more, my attention was again directed to the planet, when I was astonished

77

to find a manifest change in the <u>position</u> of the small bright spot. In the course of a few days the <u>small spot</u> gradually faded from the sight and was not seen at any subsequent observation.

"It will be noticed that Lowell speaks as if what he saw was the same thing that Mitchell saw. But if it were really a permanent ice-cliff, why did Lowell and Green see the two flashes and Mitchell one flash? Any why it something so permanent that both Green and Lowell saw it many years apart, and why did it prove so impermanent when Mitchell saw it? Why was it only one gleam then, and not two, and why did it fade away?"

A GLEAM FROM THE CENTRAL SUN OF MARS

"Obviously it was a gleam from the central sun of Mars that Mitchell saw, and the reason it faded was because cloudy weather gradually obscured the interior atmosphere of Mars. And when Green and Lowell saw it a small cloud had passed over the face of the interior sun and that broke the gleam into two projecting beams with this opacity between them, so that to Lowell two separated parts of the area of the Martian sun were visible and each sent its rays of light direct into his telescope."

"It is very interesting to read Lowell's account of these observations and to note how his observations all fit into one another and are accurate and how his explanations fail to account really for what he sees. In this same part of his book, 'MARS', he speaks of a fellow observer, Mr. Douglass, who detected RIFTS in the cap---which sounds suspiciously as if this observer has seen clouds in the interior of the planet passing across the face of the polar opening. And Lowell adds, 'On June 13 I noticed that behind the bright points the snow (he calls it) fell off shaded to this rift'-which again sounds as if clouds were gathering near the bright spots. He continues: '<u>Bright spots</u> continued to be seen at various points to the westward round the cap. Throughout these days the cap was to appear shaded on the terminator side.'

"The last sentence surely suggests that cloud formations were coming into the field of view and that whenever they thinned, the bright spots from the central sun could be seen between them.

"We may note, in passing, that Proctor, the English astronomer, also refers in his 'OTHER WORLDS THAN OUTS', to the brightness of the polar regions although he does not have the correct explanations of it."

"That more attention should be paid to this brightness of the polar regions of Mars, is emphasized by an English astronomer, W.E.Denning, who contributed to the English scientific periodical, 'NATURE', an article on the physical appearance of the planet from observations made in 1886. He says:

" 'During the past few months the north polar cap of Mars has been very bright, sometimes offering a startling contrast to those regions of the surface more feebly reflective. These luminous regions of Mars require at least as much careful investigation as the darker parts, for it is probably in connection with them that physical changes (if at present operating on the planet's surface) may be definitely observed. In many previous drawings and descriptions of Mars, sufficient weight has not been accorded to these white spots.

"Earlier writers, however, had noticed that the spots were brighter than the other surfaces of Mars, an astronomer, writing in the Scientific American Supplement as early as 1879, in effect, having made that observation. But this writer was not aware of the real nature of the light. In 1892 the celebrated English astronomer, J. Norman Lockyer, repeated in a periodical, a number of observations he had made thirty years before and had then communicated to the Royal Astronomical Society of England. Here is a significant quotation "The snow-zone was at times so bright that, like the crescent of the young moon, it appeared to project beyond the planet's limb. This effect of irradiation was frequently visible; on one occasion the snow spot was observed to shine like a nebulous star when the planet itself was obscurred by clouds, a phenomenon noticed by Messrs Beer and Madler, recorded in their valuable work, 'Fragments Sur les Corps Celestes.' The brightness, however, seemed to vary very considerably, and at times, especially when the snow zone was near its minimum, it was by no means the prominent object it generally is upon the planet's disc."

A DIRECT SOURCE OF LIGHT

"No one who reads the above in the light of our theory can fail to see how it fits into it. A snow cap would not reflect light with so much more vividness than the other surfaces of the planet, and only direct beams of light coming from a central sun could give that luminous effect above the surface of the planet and varying as the atmosphere in the interior or above it was clouded or clear. Had it been a mere ice cap, there would not have been this luminosity and, in particular, there would have been no luminosity when the planet was covered with clouds as Lockyer says it was. Furthermore, that luminosity is precisely what our aurora borealis would look like if our planet was viewed from a great distance. And the light is the same in both cases.

"From that early date we jump to 1905 and find Percival Lowell again telling of a bright white 'kernel' which he observed at the southern end of the Martian north polar cap.

"That then is the situation. All the evidence points to the fact that is in light, and direct light at that, that causes what we have called the Martian polar openings. But perhaps the reader is still not convinced. He may recall that the writers who treat this aspect of Mars, whether or not they believe in the "canals" seem to have no doubt of the fact that at the poles we have snow or ice. We have already pointed out some inconsistencies in this view. Here are some other considerations that help to dispel that idea, and then, by turning to the planet Venus, we shall demonstrate absolutely, that the polar circles are not snow, or ice, or even hoar-frost caps, but simply apertures leading to the inner and illuminated surface of the planet."

SUPPORTING FACTS FROM VENUS

"Venus is our nearest neighbor on the side nearer the sun, just as Mars is on the side farther from the sun. It is slightly less than the earth in size. F. W. Henkel, an English astronomer, writing in 'THE ENGLISH MECHANIC AND WORLD OF SCIENCE', remarks that when Venus is observed, distinct evidence of the existence of an extensive atmosphere, twice as dense as our own, is obtained, and the spectroscope shows the presence of water vapor in some abundance. The dark portion of the planet's disc (that turned away from the sun) is occasionally seen faintly illuminated, (says professor Young) recalling the aurora on earth'.

" 'The distance of Venus from the sun is only about three-quarters that of the earth, or about 67,000,000 miles, so that it receives much more heat and light than the earth, but the presence of the extensive atmosphere may balance this excessive amount.'

"Quoting E. Walter Maunder in his very authoritative book; "Are the Planets Inhabited?; he has this to say, after describing the temperatures on the planet, about the climate of Venus: 'Here then is the sufficient explanation why the topography of Venus is concealed. The atmosphere will always be abundantly charged with water-vapor, and an almost unbroken screen of clouds will be spread throughout its upper regions. Such a screen will greatly protect the planet from the full scorching of the sun, and tend to equalize the temperature of day and night, of summer and winter, of equator and poles. The temperature range will be slight, and there will be no wide expanses of polar ice.'

POLAR CAPS OF VENUS AND MARS OUGHT TO HAVE THE SAME EXPLANATION

"When we think of that, especially in consideration with the statement that the polar markings of Venus have never been seen to contract and expand at different times, it is obvious that these marks at the poles, in the case of Venus, are nothing less than the apertures through which light streams from a central sun.

"Yet the astronomers observing apertures at the poles of Mars, explain them in one way; when they observe similar apertures at the poles of Venus, they ought to explain those in the same manner. But they cannot do it, for they have postulated frozen water or frozen carbon dioxide as the cause of the polar caps of Mars, and they know there is nothing like that on Venus. So what do they say? Let Hector MacPherson answer in his book on 'The Romance of Modern Astronomy: 'Polar caps have been observed, supposed by some to be somewhat similar to those on our own planet and on Mars. Some astronomers, however, do not regard them as snow; the drawings of Schiaparaelli represent them as separated by a dark shadow, which suggests that they represent two mighty mountain systems.'

MACPHERSON'S EXPLANATION INADEQUATE

"Before going on to a very remarkable observation, we may be permitted to criticize this idea in more than one way. In the first place, as we have said, it is absurd to explain one thing--a polar cap or area-- by invoking snow in one planet or an open polar sea,

80

and in another planet, mountains. Why should mountains on Venus imitate a polar ice cap on Mars, or an ice cap on Mars look like and be placed just like a mountain range on Venus? It is not scientific to argue in any such fashion. And we may be permitted to say also that Mr. MacPherson's language is too vague here. Is he trying to say that each so-called 'mountain range' is separated from the surrounding surface of the planet by a shadow, or does he mean that one dark mountain range is separated from the other by a darker shadow--which in that case would lie all over the planet? We hope that nothing said in this book is said in such a manner as will leave the reader in doubt as to which of two possible things we may mean."

"But to follow Mr. MacPherson a little further. He quotes a French astronomer, Trouvelet, who in 1878 found the polar spots distinctly visible; 'Their surface', he wrote 'is irregular, and seems like a confused mass of <u>luminous points</u>, separated by comparatively sombre intervening spaces. This surface is undoubtedly very broken, and resembles that of a mountainous district studded with numerous peaks, or, our polar regions with numerous, ice needles brilliantly reflecting the sunshine.'"

"Our readers will at once recognize those luminous points for what they are--gleams from the central sun. Trouvelet, not knowing this, involves himself in a mass of error in trying to explain what he saw. It is obvious that he observed the polar aperture during very cloudy weather and the gleams from the central sun were just struggling through the clouds at various points--he saw those and what he took to be sombre mountain masses were really the cloud banks through which the beams were breaking and which, of course, looked very sombre by contrast. It could not have been anything else, for, as we have just seen, the cloudy atmosphere of Venus, which is dense and never lifted, would never permit any light from the sun or other outer source to reach the surface and be reflected as this French astronomer assumes it was. And even if the light could reach the polar cap of Venus, it is admitted that that polar cap is not made of ice and so there would be no such ice-like reflection as the astronomer describes.

"Here again we have a case in which the observed facts are explained by <u>our</u> theory, in which no other theory can be made to explain them, and in which, lacking our theory, the astronomers confusedly contradict each other when they try to reduce what they see to any rational explanation.

"And just to show the reader how universally our theory works, let us refer to another planet on which observations can be made of the polar openings. It is Mercury; the planet which is so near the sun that it circles around it in eighty-eight days. Of this planet, Richard A. Procter, one of the best known astronomers of the nineteenth century says: 'It may be mentioned in passing that one phenomenon of Mercury, if real, might fairly be regarded as indicating Vulcanian energies compared with which those of our own earth would be as the puny forces of a child compared with the energies of a giant. It has been supposed that a <u>certain bright spot</u> seen in the <u>black disc of Mercury when the planet is in transit</u>, indicates some sort of <u>illumination</u> either of the surface of the planet or in its <u>atmosphere</u>. In its atmosphere it can scarcely be;

81

nor could any auroral streamers on Mercury be supposed to possess
the necessary intensity of lustre. If the surface of Mercury were
glowing with the light thus supposed to have been seen, then it can
readily be shown that over hundreds of thousands of square miles,
that surface must glow with an intensity of lustre compared with
which the brightness of the lime light would be as darkness. In
fact, the lime light is absolute darkness compared with the intrinsic
lustre of the sun's surface; and the bright spot supposed to belong
to Mercury has been seen when the strongest darkening-glasses (or
other arrangements for reducing the sun's light) have been employed.
But there can be no manner of doubt that the bright spot is an
optical phenomenon only.'

JUST LIKE SUNLIGHT

"Again we agree with the observation but not with the inference.
Here is a spot of light, plainly seen through a telescope, so bright
that the observer compares it to the incandesence of a sun. It is
a much brighter light than any mere reflection could possibly give.
But we must remember that to Proctor such an appearance must have
been staggering in the extreme. He was not only not expecting it
but he was utterly unprepared to see such a phenomenon. And so he
is utterly unable to explain it. And it is a safe rule that when
you cannot explain a thing you can make what looks like an explanation by giving the thing another name. So Proctor calls this light
'an optical phenomenon only.' Well, of course, it is an optical
phenomenon, but why does he say ONLY? Everything we see is an
optical phenomenon, but we usually try to explain the optical
phenomena. A man who saw optical phenomena that was without
explanation or cause would be in a very dubious position. People
would say he was 'seeing things'--and their meaning would not be
complimentary. But we cannot assume that Proctor's eyes had played
him a trick. He was a trained astronomical observer. So what he
saw must have had some explanation or cause behind it. He cannot
have seen a 'myth' as he himself asserts.

"Now it is obvious to us that what he saw was the central sun of
Mercury beaming directly through the polar aperture, and as Mercury
is a small planet, the interior sun would be rather near the sperture,
certainly there would not be an aqueous atmosphere with clouds to
darken its beams, and so that sun would shine with exceeding brightness. And it is notable that its beams did put Proctor in mind of
the beams from the sun that shines in the heavens upon all the
planets.

"What more could be wanted than this to show that Mercury as
well as the other planets has a central sun, that such a sun is to
be met with universally? Is it not significent that beginning with
observations on Mars we are able to go on to Venus and Mercury,
apply the same tests, and get the same results? The tests, direct
observation or photographic observation. The results, the invariable
appearance of a central sun."

SOME BOOKS LISTED IN
GARDNER'S EXTENSIVE BIBLIOGRAPHY
AT END OF HIS 450 PAGE BOOK

"A Journey to the Earth's Interior" by M.R.Gardner, 1913 and reprinted in 1920. Bibliography contains only the principal work consulted and found to contain valid contributions to the solution of the problem of the earth's interior.

Bruce, William S. LL.D.,F.R.S.E. "Polar Exploration." Henry Holt and Company 1911.

Buel, J.W. "The World's Wonders as Seen by the Great Tropical and Polar Explorers". St.Louis, Mo. and Philadelphia, Pa. Historical Publishing Company, 1884.

Dick, Herman A.M. "The Marvelous Wonders of the Polar World". Richmond, Va., B.F.Johnson & Co.

Gordon, W.J. "Round About the North Pole", New York, E.P.Dutton & Company, 1907.

Greely, Adolphus W. "Three Years of Arctic Service" an Account of the Lady Franklin Bay Expedition of 1881-1884 and the"Attainment of the Farest North". New York, Charles Scribner's Sons. 1886.

Hayes, Dr.I.I. "The Open Polar Sea: a Narrative of a Voyage of Discovery Towards the North Pole in the Schooner United States". New York, Hurd and Houghton. 1867.

Kane, Elisha Kent, M.D., U.S.N. "Arctic Explorations in the years 1853, 54, 55". Philadelphia, J.B.Lippincott & Co. 1856.

Nordenskiold, Dr. N. Otto G. and Dr. Johann Gunnar Anderson, "Antarctic: or Two Years Amongst the Ice of the South Pole". London. Hurst & Blacket. New York. The Macmillan Company 1905.

Nordenskiold, Adolph Erik. "The Arctic Voyage of 1858-1879. London. Macmillan & Co. 1879.

Payer, Julius, one of the commanders of the expedition, "New Lands Within the Arctic Circle". New York. A. Appleton & Co., 1877.

Sargent, Epes. "Perils and Escapes among Icebergs." The Wonders of the Arctic World. A History of all the Researches and Discoveries in the Frozen Regions of the North from the Earliest Times". Philadelphia. John E. Potter & Co. 1873.

Scott, O. Firth, "The Romance of Polar Exploration". London. Seely Service & Co. 1915.

Miller, Hon. J. Marin: "Discovery of the North Pole: Dr. Frederick Cook's Own Story of How He Reached the North Pole, April 21, 1908 and the Story of Commander Peary's Discovery of April 6, 1909. 1909.

Nansen, Fridtjof, G.C.V.O. D.Sc. D.C.L. Ph.D. Professor of Oceanography in the University of Christiana. "In Northern Mists: Arctic Exploration in Early Times". 2 Volumes. London, William Heinemann. 1911.

Nanse, F. "The First Crossing of Greenland". 2 Volumes. London. Longemans, Green & Co. 1890.

Nansen, F. "Farthest North: Being the Record of a Voyage of Exploration of the Ship Fram 1893-1896 and of a Fifteen Months' Sleigh Journey by Dr. Nansen and Lieut. Johnson." 2 Vols. New York and London. Harper & Bros. 1898.

Nansen, F. "Farthest North". 2 Volumes. New York and London. Harper & Bros. 1879.

Seen, Dr. Nicholas. M.D., Ph.D., C.M. "In the Heart of the Arctic". Chicago. W.B.Conkey Company 1907.

Stefansson, Vilhajalmer, "My Life With the Eskimaux". New York. The MacMillan Compeny. 1913.

"Symmes' Theory of Concentric Spheres" by a Citizen of the United States. Morgan Lodge & Fisher. 1826.

TO BE ADDED TO END OF SUPPLEMENTARY MATERIAL
ON
"FLYING SAUCERS FROM THE EARTH'S INTERIOR"

Just as we finished writing this book, we received a most
remarkable communication from Dr. and Mrs. W.C. Halsey of Logan,
Utah, of their remarkable experience in the Arctic, which, if true,
confirms the basic thesis of this book, namely, that flying saucers
come from the hollow interior of the earth through the polar openings.
We quote from his report on his trip to the Arctic in search of the
opening into the Earth's interior, from where he believes the flying
saucers come:

"Recently there was a group of eight of us that took a trip
into the Arctic. We were looking for something. We were looking
for the opening into the interior of the Earth. The Earth is hollow.
Everything in creation is hollow, even the hair of your head is
hollow. And so we proceeded to Fairbanks, Alaska and the interior
of Alaska; and, after regrouping our associates and waiting for the
heavy snows and the mountain passes near Eagle, north of Fairbanks,
to clear, we began to proceed to the north.

"Part of our party followed the snowplows in,as far north as
you can drive on the North American Continent, on the Yukon River,
where is the little village of Circle, Alaska. My wife and I, and
one of our party followed four days later, and the thaws had really
begun to show up, and the frost blisters began to come up in the
road until there were ruts 18 to 20 inches deep, as wide as the
road, and sometimes 200 feet long.

"I set out on foot to see if I could find a sourdough cabin or
a miner or a trapper or someone that had some transportation that
could aid us, and the farther I walked the more I decided to give
up the whole thing, because of the circumstances of the road. I
looked up over the river and guess what I saw? There were five of
them sitting there, as clear as anything I ever saw, and at about
300 feet off the surface of the road. Within a period of a few
minutes they sat there, and then they were gone. Just like you
would turn a light off, they disappeared. We had a feeling within
our consciousness that we were not alone. We had a feeling that
this was a sign that we should go ahead.

"We arrived at our destination in the north...There we found
that the University of Alaska had exploration going on around Fort
Yukon and those places in the far north up into the area of the
Brooks Range, as far as they could travel, and there they took
what is known as snow caterpillars or snowtrains, which are enclosed
caterpillar tractors, pulling their supplies. There they would go
into an outpost, and from there they would take aircraft and fly to
a very secret camp in the north, where they were said to be doing
work for the organization that is the successor of the International
Geophysical Year scientist. They said that the nature of the work
is very secret. It is controlled by the Military, but they said
there is a lot of information that had come through, or leaked
through, stating they were very alarmed because a major phase of
exploration that our own Navy established has recently been taken
over by the Russians, and they were barring us from the entrances.

"We asked about the feasibility and the opportunity to go across this area ourselves and get as close to the opening and the interior of the Earth as we could, stating we would like to go into the interior. They said that because of the international situation, and because the Military restriction was set up as it had been, it would be impossible to proceed on to that location unless we had a pass from the Military, and also we would have to have a helicopter. We felt like we would make this attempt later.

"We have had some interesting communications with a bush pilot in this area. These are boys that can fly without a compass or map to almost any post of the interior of Alaska. Questioning him on the location of the place we wanted to go near, so that we could actually go into the interior of the Earth, we were informed that this location was closed, even to our Government officials and that the Soviet Union had taken over, just literally came over and set down and took over the exploration site. He said that in going into that area, he never did so without seeing one or more flying saucers there. He said on the first occasion, he flew out of a cloud bank and right in front of him was a stationary static object that was very round, shaped like a bell, and glowed very brightly. He said he thought he was going to run right into it, but as he approached, it rose up and he went right underneath, and then came down. Then it came up, circles around and stopped and remained stationary. He said he didn't know what it was but supposed it was what some folks call flying saucers. "It was unidentified as far as I was concerned", he said, and so I returned to Ladd A.F. Base at Fairbanks, Alaska, and I told the briefing officer there that I had spotted a UFO, what most people call flying saucer." He was ordered by military authorities to keep this secret and never report what he saw.

"We found it was quite impossible to go into this area, so we remembered that George Van Tassel in his "Proceedings", about three years ago, published information that near a very far north Air Force Base, that there was an opening into the interior of the Earth. We decided to look for that entrance, so a group of us circled out to the wilderness around one side of this Air Force installation, on Government land, and we struck upon a road that was well traveled, but seemed to be more or less a restricted road. It said, "Government Property, KEEP OUT!"

"We were able to gleen a lot of information from the Indians. The Indians have a tradition which they pass down from. They state that their origin was from the north. We asked how far north, and they said you don't understand. They drew a circle as it were a great opening, or a big hole in the surface of the Earth; and they said: "We came out of the north," meaning from the opening in the north."

Commenting on the above statements by Dr. Halsey, it should be remembered that the North Polar opening is quite large and is at the geometrical North Pole and not in Alaska.

THE AGHARTAN EXPEDITION AND THE AGHARTAN ORDER

After three years of searching in Brazil for an opening to the Subterranean World, the author of this book has come to the conclusion that it is not necessary to search for the subterranean cities of the Atlanteans in the Roncador Mountains of Matto Grosso as Colonel Fawcett did, since the states of Santa Catarina and Parana, Brazil are honeycombed by a network of Atlantean tunnels that lead to subterranean cities. These tunnels represent stupendous engineering feats by a master race. The writer is now organizing an expedition, known as the Aghartan Expedition, for the purpose of investigating these tunnels, with the object of reaching the subterranean cities to which they lead, after which he hopes to establish contact with the still-living members of the Elder Race of Atlanteans and arrange for bringing qualified persons to them to establish residence in their cities in a World Free from Fallout and thus avoid radioactive destruction which will eventually be the fate of all surface dwellers.

In a letter that appeared in "Flying Saucers" magazine, Wm. L. Constantine writes:

"For many years it has been my opinion that a race of highly intelligent people do actually live in the Earth's core...If Admiral Byrd did not find this lush 74 degree climate at the Pole in 1947, is it not a more than reasonable assumption that our government would make a great effort to follow through? Byrd says he was forced to turn back after 2300 miles because of a dwindling gas supply. Granting this be true, this problem no longer exists. If my information is correct we have planes which can do far better now...I believe that has already been done and that landings have been made and contacts firmly established on a sound and lasting basis...Can it be that our government is trying to lull the rest of the world?"

THE TRUTH ABOUT ADMIRAL BYRD'S FLIGHT TO
THE UNKNOWN LAND BEYOND THE POLE

The theories of Reed and Gardener presented in this book found confirmation in Admiral Byrd's historical air trips <u>beyond</u> both North and South Poles into the Polar openings that lead to the hollow interior of the earth. In the February 1961 issue of "FLYING SAUCERS" appears an article "'BYRD DID MAKE NORTH POLE FLIGHT IN FEB. 1947' - GIANNINI", which starts with the following statement by the editor, Ray Palmer:

"The question being placed before the readers of FLYING SAUCERS at the present moment is not whether or not the Earth is hollow and that openings exist at both poles, or whether it is otherwise shaped and extends into space at the poles (Giannini's theory), but whether or not Admiral Byrd actually flew over the North Pole in February, 1947 and whether or not he 'penetrated 1700 miles <u>beyond</u> it' into an unknown land area which does not exist on present-day maps. Therefore, we present the following letters as evidence, and we will let both of them stand on their own merits."

Mr. Ogden writes:

"On July 23rd I wrote another letter to Mr. Giannini asking him to give an account of himself about Admiral Byrd and what The New York Times reports. I asked him your question about why he tried to destroy his theory by including a fictional flight by Byrd to the North Pole in 1947."

The following is then quoted from a letter by Giannini to Mr. Ogden:

"The author was extended courtesy, by the New York office of U.S. Naval Research, to transmit a redio message of godspeed to Rear Admiral Richard Evelyn Byrd, U.S.N., at his Arctic base in February, 1947.

"At that time the late Rear Admiral Byrd announced through the press, 'I'd like to see the land beyond the pole; that area <u>beyond the Pole is the center of the great unknown</u>.' Subsequently Admiral Byrd; and a naval task force, executed a seven hour flight, of 1700 miles, over land extending beyond the theorized North Pole 'end' of the Earth.

"In January, 1947, and prior to the flight, this author was enabled to sell a series of newspaper features to an international feature syndicate only because of this author's assurance to the syndicate director that <u>Byrd would in fact go beyond the imaginary North Pole point</u>.

"As a result of this author's prior knowledge of the then commonly unknown land extending beyond the pole points, and after the syndicated features had been released in the press, this author was widely investigated by the Office of the U.S. Naval Intelligence. That Intelligence investigation stemmed from the fact of Byrd's definite confirmation of this author's revolutionizing disclosures.

"Later, March, 1958, this author delivered a radio address in Missouri, expressing the import of land discovered beyond the imaginary

North Pole and South Pole points of archaic theory.

"As concerns your own too hasty observations, be informed that this author made no 'blunder' of fact, nor did he in any manner 'destroy' his book, as you so wrongfully assert.

"Neither you, nor Paomer, nor his reading audience, know where Rear Admiral Richard Evelyn Byrd was during the entire month of February 1947. But the conservative and revealing Times accounts recently transmitted to you (and which you did not want to see) should afford a more intelligent appraisal for your own benefit."

Giannini speaks of other New York publications carrying an account of Byrd's 1947 trip beyond the North Pole, which the Times did not print, and comments:

"Those accounts described Byrd's 1700 mile flight, of seven hours over land and fresh water lakes BEYOND the assumptive North Pole 'end' of the Earth. And the dispatches were intensified until a strict censorship was imposed from Washington.

"Concerning your issue with Palmer's contention that Byrd flew 1700 miles beyond the South Pole, you should now have realized that the 1700 miles applied to the North Pole. But, and this little morsel you can believe or reject, as you will, Rear Admiral George Dufek, acting under Admiral Byrd, accomplished a flight of 2,300 miles beyond the South Pole on January 13, 1956. Does that little feature disturb? It fails to disturb members of Naval Intelligence with whom this author has spoken since the occasion."

PUBLICATIONS OF HEALTH RESEARCH, 70 Lafayette St., MOKELUMNE HILL, CALIFORNIA 95245
(This is a partial list - send .50 for large 8½ x 11, magazine type catalogue of
complete (approximately 500) listings - always in stock! 50¢ refundable on $5.00
purchase. Books have Soft Paper Covers. LISTED BY AUTHOR(if several authors - by
subject). 15% Discount Given on $25.00 Orders (sent at one time - to one address in
U.S. & Possessions (Only). No Discount on Foreign Orders (where frequently extra
postage is necessary & insurance expensive - in many cases unobtainable!) Discount
allowed only if you'll give us your zip code, if you have purchased before (and
enclose complete face of the last third class mailing envelope - which to us gives
a key to name in our 100,000 customer file - preventing future duplication mailing
to customers. Order $25.00 Worth & Remit $21.25...adding 50¢ for Postage & ins. On
Complete Order ($21.75). California Residents Add 4% Sales Tax. (For more details
on the publications get our 50¢ catalogue!)

AURA & WHAT IT MEANS TO YOU (1955 copyright) - A Compilation from the best
    authorities on the subject - 108 indexed 8½ x 11 pages, mimeographed,
    printed cover $3.50
Baughan, Rosa - THE INFLUENCE OF THE STARS - 272 pages, ills., spirals (1904)4.00
Chase, J. Munsell - THE RIDDLE OF THE SPHINX (1915) - 86 pages - highly ills 2.00
Christian, Eugene - UNCOOKED FOODS (1904 copyright) 246 ind. pages, spirals 2.50
COLOR HEALING - An Exhaustive Survey Compiled from the 21 works of the leading
    Practitioners of Chromotherapy (1956), including a condensation of the
    rare book, Principles of Light & Color by Edwin D. Babbitt, M.D. - 161
    indexed, mimeographed pages, printed cover   5.00
Crone, Prof. J. O. - THE MAGNETIC HEALER'S GUIDE (1903 copyright) - 125 pages
    Spirals   2.50
DIABETES - By Drs. Brady, Tilden, White, Weger & Shelton. 8½ x 11 (1965) -
    Mimeographed - 40 pages   1.50
Dickhoff, Dr. Robert Ernst - AGHARTA (1951) - 106 pages, spirals   3.00
Dickhoff, Dr. Robert Ernst - HOMECOMING OF THE MARTIANS (1958) 175 pages   3.00
Dickhoff, Dr. Robert Ernst - THE ETERNAL FOUNTAIN - 129 pages, highly ills.,
    spirals   3.00
Dowd, F. B. - REGENERATION (Being Part II of the Temple of the Rosy Cross) -
    Rosicrucian Philosophy (1900) 1964 reprint - 144 pages, spirals   2.00
Drayton, H. S. (M.D.) - HUMAN MAGNETISM Its Nature, Physiology and Psychology
    (1889 copyright) - 66 pages, mimeographed, 8½ x 11   3.00
Emerson, Willis - THE SMOKY GOD (or, A Voyage to the Inner World) (1908 copy-
    right) Reprinted 1965 (Impossible to locate in any library) 9 full-page
    illustrations in black & white - 186 pages - spirals - large print   4.00
Fletcher, Ella Adelia - THE LAW OF THE RHYTHMIC BREATH (1908) - 372 ind.
    pages, spirals (large print)   4.00
Gauvin, Marshall J. - THE STRUGGLE BETWEEN RELIGION AND SCIENCE (1932) Reprint
         1.00
Gordon, Rev. Edward - OUR LIFE AFTER DEATH - 223 pages, Prologue & Epilogue by
    Prof. Hilton Hotema - spiral binding   3.00
Guthrie, Kenneth Sylvan (M.D.) - THE GOSPEL OF APOLLONIUS OF TYANA - (1965
    reprint) 73 pages, spirals - illustrated   2.00
Handall, Frank H. - PRIVATE VITAL MAGNETIC POWER (Mesmerism), Hypnotism &
    Thought-Reading - 57 mimeographed 8½ x 11 pages   1.50
Hanish, Dr. Otoman Zar-Adusht - INNER STUDIES - A Course of 12 Lessons - spi-
    rals - 206 indexed pages   4.00
Hanish, Dr. Otoman Zar-Adusht - HEALTH AND BREATH CULTURE - According to Maz-
    daznan Philosophy (Sun-Worship) - Ills. , 121 8½ x 11 pages (new price) 3.00
Hinton, C. H. - THE FOURTH DIMENSION (1906) Colored Plate, Diagrams. The
    Fourth Dimension is Now Coming Into Its Own and This Rare Reprint Will
    Be Most Welcome By The Serious Student. 247 pages, spirals   3.50
Khei (Rosicrucian) - A BRIEF COURSE IN MEDIUMSHIP - 79 pages, spirals   2.50
Mead, G. R. S. - DID JESUS LIVE 100 YEARS B.C.? 440 large ind. pages, spiral 5.00

McCarty, Burke - SUPPRESSED TRUTH - ASSASSINATION OF LINCOLN (1922) Ills.
    with photos - 272 pages - spirals $4.00

Mead, G. R. S. - APOLLONIUS OF TYANA - The Philosopher-Reformer of the First
    Century, A.D. - Offset print, 159 pages - spiral bound   3.00

Landone, Brown - YOUR EYES - REJUVENATING THEM - A Course of 29 Lessons -
    47 8½ x 11 pages, offset, typewritten format - ills. Printed Covers   3.00

Landone, Brown - MYSTERIOUS CATALYTIC FOODS - Mimeographed - 63 pages   2.50

Landone, Brown - TRUTH AND ITS MAGNIFICIENT SIMPLICITY - 62 8½ x 11 pages,
    offset, typewritten format   2.50

Peeke, Margaret - ZENIA THE VESTAL - An Occult Novel Based on Occult Laws -
    spirals (1896)   5.00

Pitzer, Geo. C. (M.D.) - SUGGESTION IN THE CURE OF DISEASES And The Correct-
    ion of Vices (1899 - 4th ed.) 80 indexed pages, offset, spirals   4.00

Randolph, Dr. Paschal Beverly (M.D. - Rosicrucian) - AFTER DEATH THE DISEMBODI-
    MENT OF MAN - (1886) Reprinted 1961 - 161 8½ x 11 pages   3.00

Randolph, Dr. P. B. - SOUL - THE SOUL-WORLD: The Homes of the Dead (Reprinted
    1961) - 128 8½ x 11 mimeographed pages   3.00

Randolph, Dr. P. B. - RAVALETTE THE ROSICRUCIAN'S STORY - Reprinted 1960 -
    108 8½ x 11 indexed pages (new price)   3.00

Randolph, Dr. P. B. - EULIS - The History of Love (1874) Reprinted 1961 - 139
    8½ x 11 mimeographed pages, printed covers   3.00

Randolph, Dr. P. B. - DEALINGS WITH THE DEAD: The Human Soul, Its Migrations
    and Its Transmigrations (1861-62) Reprinted 1959 - mimeographed - 156
    8½ x 11 pages, printed, ills. cover   3.00

RAPHAEL'S HORARY ASTROLOGY - Reprint - 103 pages, spiral binding   1.50

Reichenbach, Charles Von - PHYSICO-PHYSIOLOGICAL RESEARCHES ON THE DYNAMICS OF
    MAGNETISM, ELECTRICITY, HEAT, LIGHT, CRYSTALLIZATION, AND CHEMISM. (1965
    reprint) Facsimile of first American Edition 1851. Spiral bound -
    456 pages   10.00

REICHENBACH'S LETTERS ON OD AND MAGNETISM (1852) - The Odic Theory - Spirals
    - 119 pages   5.00

Richardson, Dr. R. A. - REMOVING FACIAL WRINKLES - 110 pages, spirals   2.00

Scott, Cyril - THE CHRISTIAN PARADOX - 144 pages (fine print) spirals   3.50

Schure, Edouard - PYTHAGORAS (Reprinted 1964) - 180 pages - spirals   3.00

Sepharial - THE SILVER KEY (A Guide to Speculators) 94 pages, ills., spirals 3.00

Stein, Henry Binkley - THIRTY THOUSAND GODS BEFORE JEHOVAH (1940 copyright)
    90 mimeographed pages, 8½ x 11   2.00

Stein, Henry Binkley - THE AXE WAS GOD (The Jackal Occupies The Center of
    The Zodiac) - 44 indexed, mimeographed 8½ x 11 pages   1.50

Steiner, Dr. Rudolph - GATES OF KNOWLEDGE - 121 pages, spirals   2.00

Steiner, Dr. Rudolph - THE MISSION OF SPIRITUAL SCIENCE   1.00

Stewart, Basil - THE GREAT PYRAMID (1927) - 78 pages with diagrams.   1.50

NICOLA TESLA - FORGOTTEN SUPERMAN - Photograph, offset, typewritten format
    (Copyright by Ralph Bergstresser) (Printed by Special Permission) 15
    pages (3 for $1.00) each   .35

TUBERCULOSIS By J. H. Tilden, M.D., William H. Hay, M.D., F. W. Collins,
    George Starr White, M.D., Herbert M. Shelton, N.D., Wm. F. Koch, M.D. -
    8½ x 11, Mimeographed, 37 pages   2.00

Vail, Isaac Newton - THE MISREAD RECORD Or The Deluge and Its Cause   2.00

Walton, Page - NAMES DATES & NUMBERS - System of Numerology (1914)   2.00

Wattles, Wallace D. - FINANCIAL SUCCESS THROUGH CREATIVE THOUGHT (or, The
    Science of Getting Rich) (1927) 155 pages plus added questions,answers   3.00

Wigston, W. F. C. - HERMES STELLA Or Notes and Jottings Upon the Bacon Cipher
    (1890) - 182 pages (1965 reprint)   4.00

Winbigler, Dr. C. F. - HAND BOOK OF INSTRUCTIONS FOR HEALING AND HELPING OTHERS
    (1916) Plus MANUAL OF THE LEAGUE OR CLASS OF HEALING - apprcx 180 pages,
    spirals (price increase effective July 10, 1965)   3.00

MacHuisdean, W. Hamish, - THE GREAT LAW (Vol. I - First Two Visits) - Offset
    reproduction (8½ x 11) Illustrated Cover and text. 53 pages   1.50

MIMEOGRAPHED FOLIOS - $40.00 Worth for $30.00 Prepaid
(8 Sets of Budget Answers With Each $30.00 Received).

California Residents Kindly Add 4% Sales Tax - Thank You.
HEALTH RESEARCH, MOKELUMNE HILL, CALIFORNIA.

Human Magnetism - H. S. Drayton, M.D. Gives much data on Animal
    Magnetism or Hypnotism (rare). $2.50

The Philosophy Of Human Life - Isaac Jennings, M.D. (1852). With special
    Design to Develop the True Idea of Diseases; Its Nature, Immediate Oc-
    casion, and General Remedy. We sold the original for $25.00 - now in
    mimeographed form   4.00

Health Reformer Gleanings - Compiled By Marcia Terrell (7th Day Adventist &
    Natural Hygienist) from old issues of the original health journal of the
    Seventh-Day Adventists, "The Health Reformer" magazine. The subjects
    covered are not only timely and up-to-date, in many respects, but show a
    wealth of humor and sturdy strength characteristic of these early Hygienists.
    The pioneers understood many things that have been forgotten by present
    day health minded people.

      While this is published primarily for the Seventh-Day Adventists,
    vegetarians & Natural Hygienists - others interested in health, truth and
    the simple way of life will enjoy this unique folio of health truths.

      The folio covers the following (which are the concepts of the various
    authors): Hygienic Diet by R. T. Trall, M.D.; Jaundice, How to Cure Colds,
    A Word to Christian Mothers by E. G. White; Health by Elder D. T. Bordeau;
    Drug Medication by Mrs. E. G. White; Dress Reform by Mrs. E. G. White;
    Exercise for Invalids; Excerpts from "The Laws of Life"; Air and Sunshine;
    Parents Their Own Physician by Mrs. E. G. White; Principles of Hygienic
    Medication by R. T. Trall, M.D.; About Dr. R. T. Trall, M. D., By James
    White; Bible Hygiene - James White; The Health Reform Institute; The Fun-
    damental Principles of the Hygienic System; Small-Pox; The Want of Hygienic
    Knowledge; Too Much Medicine by R. T. Trall, M.D.; The Sins of the Par-
    ents; Two Meals a Day by James White; Reformers; How to Live: A History of
    James White; Florence Nightingale; Exercise by Mrs. E. G. White; Dress and
    Circulation by James White; Childrens' Dress by Mrs. E. G. White; Inflam-
    mation of the lungs; Life in the Rocky Mounts by E. G. White; Summer in the
    Rocky Mountains by James White; Cocoa Drink; Old Maids; Vegetable Fats;
    The Apostasy of Solomon; Experience by E. G. White; Words to Christian
    Mothers; The Hygienic Festival etc. Flexible covers -   1.50

TEA AND COFFEE: Their Physical, Intellectual, and Moral Effects on the Human
    System - by Dr. William A. Alcott.
TEA AND COFFEE - Are They Injurious - Some Substitutes for Both - By Kate J.
    Jackson, M.D.
HOW TO TAKE BATHS - By Miss Harriet N. Austin, M.D. (written in 1869)
HOW TO NURSE THE SICK - By James C. Jackson, M.D. (1868)
DYSPEPSIA AND ITS TREATMENT - By James C. Jackson, M.D. (1876)
    ALL of the above was written around 1860-69 are now rare and out of print. These
    several booklets and pamphlets have been combined into one mimeographed
    folio for those who are interested in Natural Hygiene. In fact we've sold the
    rare booklet on Tea and Coffee by itself for $6.00. Our price for this mimeo-
    graphed folio (which includes all of the above titles) only -   2.00

MIMEOGRAPHED FOLIOS
$40.00 Sent At One Time For Only $30.00 Postpaid (with any 8 sets of budget answers).

THE MASONIC LOST WORD By G. V. Tudhope. (Off-set, varityped manuscript, 6
    pages). Freemasons have failed to recognize that it was the fear of Bacon's inter-
    pretations of THAT WORD becoming accepted that caused Pope Clement XII, in
    1738, and succeeding Popes thereafter to denounce and condemn Free-Masonry $ .30

HYPNOSIS -- NERVOUS AND MENTAL DISEASES, MONOGRAPHED - Translated From
    The German - By Paul Schilder, M.D., and Dr. Otto Kauders, Assistant of the
    Psychiatric Clinic, Vienna, Translated by Simon Rothenberg, M.D., attending
    Neurologist. The Jewish and Israel-Zion Hospitals, Brooklyn, N.Y. 118 p.   4.00

ELEMENTARY RADIESTHESIA & THE USE OF THE PENDULUM - By V. D. Wethered,
    B.Sc., the world's foremost expert (England). Illustrated by professional full
    page drawings, order now. Illustrated cover. Mimeographed 8-1/2 x11.   1.50

SEERSHIP OR SOUL SIGHT - Paschal Beverly Randolph, M.D. We have mimeographed
    this rare gem by this famous Rosicrucian, author & teacher. Dr. Randolph visited
    Egypt, Arabia, Syria, Palestine, Turkey, Greece and other nations - he was re-
    ceived in the inner circles - and was given the privilege of scanning the pages
    of the most secret manuscripts, as well as the right to initiation into all the
    rites of the various orders. He met such men as Hargrave Jennings, Lord Lytton,
    Mackenzie, Eliphas Levi, Alexander Dumas, etc. Now brought to you in
    mimeographed form.   2.00

REGENERATION - Sidney Weltmer - A discussion of the Sex Question from a New
    and Scientific Standpoint (1898) - Mimeographed reprint.   2.00

COMMUNISM IN AMERICA - One of the hottest books of 1961 (off-set printed,
    illustrated with photos and rare, secret documents and mimeographed)
    durable flexible printed cover. Don't miss it - tomorrow may be too late!   3.00

WHAT IS TRUTH - our own compilation on fluoridation, drugs, processed foods,
    natural treatments of cancer, cancer cures, government agencies. Over 300
    8-1/2 x 11 pages, photo copies, off-set and mimeographed of hard to find docu-
    ments which were NOT intended for public consumption. These subjects will
    not be found in your library and will not be taught in public schools - nor will
    your doctor tell you about them. A Must! Over 1,000 copies sold and many are
    using this for group study - sold on a money-back guarantee - and only one
    person has ever returned the book to us! Fully indexed. This is a shocking book
    about the untruths told in public mediums - learn the truth and be free!   2.00

DREAMS - By C. W. Leadbeater. What They Are and How They Are Caused. Phy-
    sical, Etheric, Astral, The Ego, The Brain, The Esoteric Brain, Astral Body,
    Ego in Sleep, The True Vision, The Prophetic Dream, The Symbolical Dream,
    The Vivid and Connected Dream and the Confused Dream. Conclusion.   1.50

WHICH BIBLE - The hottest book ever written - money back guarantee - shows
    why the revised, standard edition of the King James Bible has been rewritten
    by the Communists plus many secret documents, never released by the
    newspapers. (Mimeographed and off-set).   3.00

A COMPILATION OF THE BEST OF THE VARIOUS BOOKS ON THE SUBJECT OF YOGA
    By a deep student. Mimeographed, printed covers. 42 exercises, Illustrated.
    We believe this is one of the finest books on this subject obtainable - many
    have ordered 10 and 50 copies to present to friends and students.   2.00

HEALTH RESEARCH, MOKELUMNE HILL, CALIFORNIA.

A JOURNEY TO THE EARTH'S INTERIOR - Or Have The Poles Really Been
Discovered - By Marshall B. Gardner - Revised and Enlarged Edition. Published by
the author at Aurora, Ill. (1920). 456 pages, soft covers, spiral binding (a photographic reprint, 1964) - $5.00

This facsimile reproduction will be most welcome to the readers of Flying Saucer
books. This will be especially true to those who have read the three Dr. Raymond
Bernard publications. All of the interesting illustrations have been reproduced with
good detail. Limited edition - get your copy now! (Original, used copies have gone
at $15.00 each in the past, now it is nearly impossible to locate an original copy).

CONTENTS: (Chapter Headings): The Nebula and Our Theory; Introductory; Mars;
Early Polar Exploration; Further Arctic Exploration; Greely's Exploration; Nordenski-
old's Voyages; With Nansen in the North; Was the North Pole Discovered?; Two
Congressional Opinions on Peary and Cook; The Mammoth; The Life of the Arctic;
Other Interesting Animals of the Interior; The Aurora; The Eskimo; Evidence in the
Antarctic; The Journey to the Earth's Interior; The Formation of the Earth; How Our
Theory Differs From That of Symmes; The Moon; A Note on Gravitation; How Our Theory
has been Received; Our Controversey With Dominian; Our Country and Our Theory;
In Conclusion. 12 pages of Illustrations.
  This 1964 photographic reproduction, spiral bound, soft covers - $5.00.

*****   *****   *****   *****   *****   *****   *****   *****

  THE PHANTOM OF THE POLES - By William Reed. (1906 copyright) Soft covers,
Spirals, 283 pages, illustrated. The author says this volume was not written to
entertain those who read for amusement, but to establish and prove, so far as proof
can be established and proved, a half-score or more of mighty truths hitherto not
comprehended. This may seem boastful; but, when understood, I hope it will not be
so considered; for one key will unlock them all.

The problems to be solved are as follows (says the author of this volume):

(1) Why is the earth flattened at the poles? (2) Why have the poles never been reached?
(3) Why is the sun invisible so long in winter near the farthest points north or south?
(4) What is the Aurora Borealis? (5) Where are icebergs formed, and how? (6) What
produces a tidal wave? (7) Why do meteors fall more frequently near the poles, and
whence do they come? (8) What causes the great ice-pressure in the Arctic Ocean
during still tide and calm weather? (9) Why is there colored snow in the Arctic region?
(10) Why is it warmer near the poles than six hundred to one thousand miles away from
them? (11) Why is ice in the Arctic Ocean frequently filled with rock, gravel, sand,
etc.? (12) Does the compass refuse to work near the poles?

CONTENTS : Introduction; General Summary; Flattening of the Earth at the Poles; Length
of Polar Nights; Working of the Compass; Around the Curve; Mysteries of the Polar
Regions; The Water-sky; What it Is; The Aurora: Its Wonderful Variations; Meteors or
Volcanic Disturbances; Finding of Rock in and On Ice; Dust in the Arctic; Open Water
at the Farthest Point North and South; Why It Is Warmer Near the Poles; Driftwood--
Whence It Came; Have Others Than Esquimos Inhabited the Arctic Regions?; What
(Over Please)

Produces Colored Snow in the Arctic?; Where and How Are Ice-Bergs Formed?;
The Tidal Wave; Clouds, Fogs, and Vapors; Arctic and Antarctic Winds; The Centre
of Gravity; Cannot Reach the Poles (this was written in 1906); What Is The Interior
of The Earth?; In Conclusion.

Send $5.00 now for this amazing volume.

***** ***** ***** ***** ***** ***** ***** *****

PARADISE FOUND - Wm. F. Warren - A Study of the Prehistoric World - (The
Cradle of the Human Race At The North Pole) - First Copyright 1885. Respectfully
Dedicated with friendly permission, to Professor F. Max Muller, of the University
of Oxford. 505 indexed pages - illustrations. Soft Covers, Spiral Binding - (Reprinted 1964) (The original cloth bound book was sold at $25.00). Facsimile, Photo-
graphic Reproduction - $6.00.

The author says this book is not the work of a dreamer. It is a thoroughly
serious and sincere attempt to present what is to the author's mind the true and final
solution of one of the greatest and most fascinating of all problems connected with
the history of mankind.

That this true solution has not been furnished before is not strange. The suggestion that primitive Eden was at the Arctic Pole seems at first sight the most incredible of all wild and willful paradoxes.

CONTENTS (Chapter Headings): The Location of Eden: State of the Question;
The Results of Explorers, Historic and Legendary; The Results of Theologians; The
Results of Non-Theological Scholars; Naturalists, Ethnologists, Etc.; A Fresh Hypo-
thesis: Primitive Eden at the North Pole; The Hypothesis and the Conditions of Its
Admissibility; Important New Features at Once Introduced Into the Problem of the
Site of Eden and the Significance of These for a Valid Solution; The Hypothesis Sci-
entifically Tested and Confirmed; The Testimony of Scientific Geogony; The Testimony of Astronomical Geography; The Testimony of Physiographical Geology; The
Testimony of Prehistoric Climatology; The Testimony of Palentological Botany; The
Testimony of Palentological Zoology; The Testimony of Paleontological Anthropology
and General Ethnology; Conclusion of Part Third; The Hypothesis Confirmed by Eth-
nic Tradition; Ancient Cosmology and Mythical Geography; The Cradle of the Race
in Ancient Japanese Thought; The Cradle of the Race in Chinese Thought; The Cradle
of the Race in East Aryan or Hindu Thought; The Cradle of the Race in Iranian or Old-
Persian Thought; Further Verifications of the Hypothesis Based Upon a Study of the
Peculiarities of a Polar Paradise. Etc., Etc.

Includes Many Illustrations. This rare gem - only - $6.00.

California Residents Please Add 4% Sales Tax - Thank You.

HEALTH RESEARCH
MOKELUMNE HILL
CALIFORNIA 95245

DEPARTMENT OF DEFENSE
Office of Public Information
Washington 25, D. C.

26 January 1953

Henry Holt & Company
383 Madison Ave.
New York 17, New York.

Dear Sirs:

This will acknowledge your letter of recent date regarding a proposed book on 'flying saucers' by Major Donald E. Keyhoe, U.S. Marine Corps, retired.

We in the Air Force recognize Major Keyhoe as a responsible, accurate reporter. His long association and cooperation with the Air Force, in our study of unidentified flying objects, qualifies him as a leading civilian authority on this investigation.

All the sighting reports and other information he listed have been cleared and made available to Major Keyhoe from Air Technical Intelligence records, at his request.

The Air Force, and its investigating agency, "Project Blue-book", are aware of Major Keyhoe's conclusion that the "Flying Saucers" are from another planet. The Air Force has never denied that this possibility exists. Some of the personnel believe that there may be some strange natural phenomena completely unknown to us, but that if the apparently controlled maneuvers reported by competent observers are correct, then the only remaining explanation is the interplanetary answer.

SAYS SAUCERS REAL — Dr. Carl Jung, Swiss psychologist, says unidentified flying objects are real and "show signs of intelligent guidance by quasi-human pilots." Dr. Jung, who started his research on aerial phenomena in 1944, released his report through Holloman Air Force base center at Alamagordo, N.M. (AP Wirephoto)

Very Truly Yours
Albert M. Chop
Air Force Press Desk.

THE ABOVE LETTER has been taken from the book, HOMECOMING OF THE MARTIANS By Dr. Robert Ernst Dickhoff, Ph.D., an Encyclopaedic Work on Flying Saucers. Many actual happenings are quoted in this amazing volume which science cannot explain. Scores of photographs and unusual, rare photographs from many lands. Don't miss this wonderful volume (1964 reprint) - $3.00.

HOMECOMING OF THE MARTIANS - Dr. Robert Ernst Dickhoff,Ph.D. - soft covers, spirals - 175 pages - with scores of full page photographs. $3.00

AGHARTA - The illustrated book by Robert Ernst Dickhoff, Ph.D., Sungma Red Lama, Messenger of Buddha, Mystic, Adept. Soft covers, spirals - with rare, unusual photographs. Tells of the Colony of the Outsiders, who keep watch in "Saucers" over the progress of Mankind - today as in eons in the past. 106 pages, soft covers (the extra rare photographs make this book very valuable - a reprint of an earlier edition. Spiral binding $3.00

November 11, 1964

The Hollow Earth
Dr. Raymond Bernard
Health Research
Mokelhumne Hill, California

Dear Doctor Bernard,

I am writing this letter, having in mind two purposes. One, to order your book; second, to speak of it.

For three years now, I have known about the city within the earth, under the North Pole. In fact, I know a man that has been there. His name is Elvan Deeter. Mr. Deeter and I have tried to get the means to make the journey, either with a twenty-nine foot sloop, or with a twin-engine sea plane having a capacity of twenty-five hundred miles, fuel range. We have not yet succeeded; in fact, I came to Alaska to write a book about it and raise the funds, but you have already beat me to it, and I congratulate you.

Now, the fact is this. Brother Elvan, as I call him, knows the entrance that leads to the City Within the Earth, under the North Pole and he calls it "THE LAND OF THE PURPLE ETHER" or, "THE LAND OF THE LIVING."

In the cities of this land, the people live to 900 and 1000 years. Their average height is between twelve to seventeen feet. They are highly civilized.

If what I have said here, interests you, write to me and I shall give you information in detail. Soon the entrance of this land might be closed indefinitly. If you are interested to go there, then we must hurry.

Enclosed is $4.00 for a copy of your book. Please send it Airmail.

If you are really sincere, please write to me immediately. We must no longer waste time.

Respectfully yours,

John Nazarian

John Nazarian

JN:kn

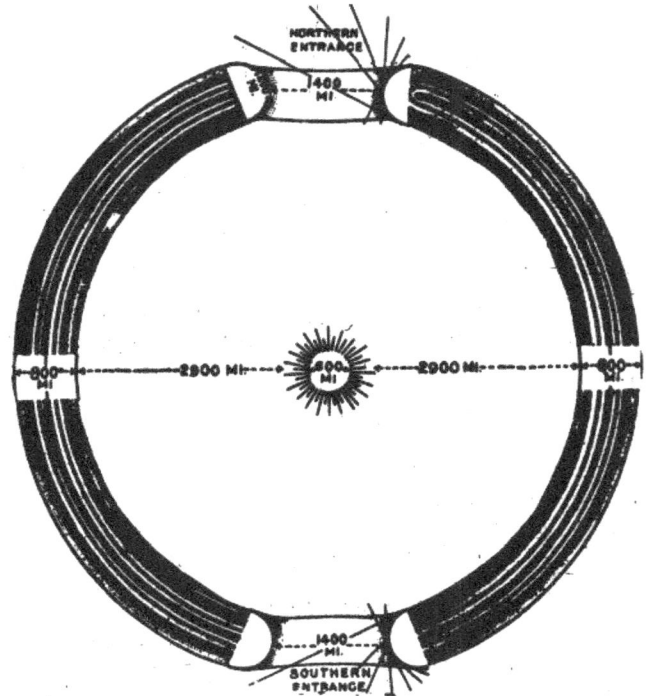

1 & 2. The two diagrams above appeared in a book titled: "A Journey To The Earth's Interior". It was published in 1929 by Marshall B. Gardner. Diagrams show the earth as a hollow sphere with polar openings and a small central sun.

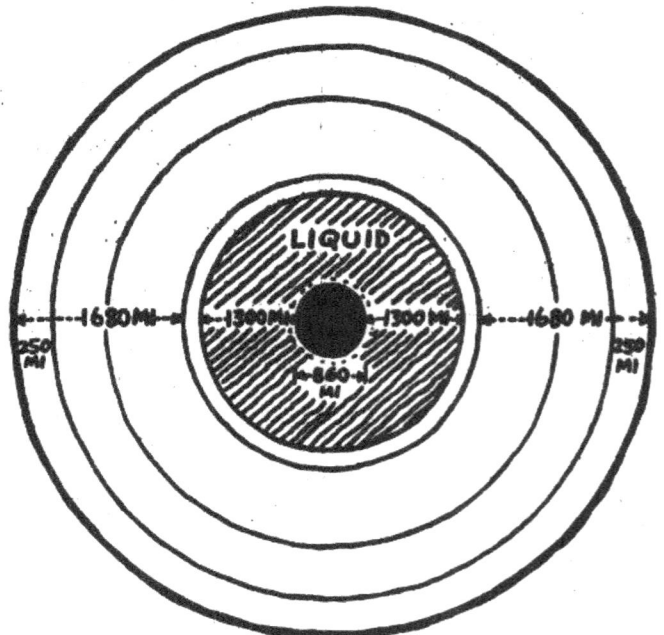

3. Ancient Teachings claim that a great "Cavern World" exists.

4. 1958 findings of modern IGY scientist explorers.

From "Rainbow City and the Inner Earth People" by Michael X, Futura Press, Box 38594, Los Angeles 38, California.

www.ingramcontent.com/pod-product-compliance
Lightning Source LLC
Chambersburg PA
CBHW081158270326
41930CB00014B/3203